THE POWER OF DESPERATION

ENDORSEMENTS

This book has a solid backbone and a tender heart, exactly what we need when things are falling apart around us. These chapters are biblical and practical but not preachy. No matter what your difficulties may be today, there's an encouraging word for you in these pages. Open the book, open your heart, and start moving toward victory.

> —Warren W. Wiersbe
> **Former pastor, The Moody Church**
> **Author of the *BE* series of Bible studies**

In these pages Michael Catt skillfully immortalizes the obvious. We often accept the obvious without struggle, resistance, or understanding, thus we seldom find victory with it. For many there is just no way out. With these pages Michael indelibly etches in our hearts the stark reality of desperation that each of us will encounter in our lifetimes and points the way to victory. This book is the road map to overcome the attacks of desperation in our lives.

> —James T. Draper, Jr.
> **President Emeritus, LifeWay Christian Resources**

In a day when things seem so very desperate and flawed, Michael Catt reminds us that God also loves very desperate and flawed people.

> —Dr. John D. Hull
> **President and CEO, EQUIP**

It's counterintuitive that wholeness comes from brokenness. Healing comes from admitting your desperate need. Want to experience life on a higher level? Then get lower. Michael Catt delivers a powerful message of God's transforming work in the heart of a Christian in the wilderness. Want to get to the other side of the crisis that you're facing? Don't try to avoid it or escape it; go *through it* with God. This is a great encouragement for every believer in Jesus Christ.

  —James MacDonald
  Pastor, Harvest Bible Church, Chicago

When our heart's desperation exceeds the desperate condition in which we live . . . revival is imminent. There is a redemptive quality in desperation, when we humbly and wholly surrender to God, allowing Him to draw us to Himself and to conform us to the image of the great Reviver, Jesus Christ. Michael Catt amazingly and transparently unveils another paradoxical principle of the Christian life, which may very well be a pathway to the next great awakening.

  —Byron Paulus
  President, Life Action Ministries

Michael Catt pulls no punches. He gets down to the root of the powerless church: we are not desperate for God, and we are not broken over sin. This message is desperately needed and will resonate deeply with every heart that is hungry for God and for revival. A powerful call to true, biblical Christianity.

  —Nancy Leigh DeMoss
  Best-selling author, *Revive Our Hearts* radio host

THE POWER OF DESPERATION

BREAKTHROUGHS IN OUR BROKENNESS

MICHAEL CATT

NASHVILLE, TENNESSEE

978-0-8054-4867-2
B&H Publishing Group
Nashville, Tennessee
www.BHPublishingGroup.com

Dewey Decimal Classification: 248.86
Despair / Hope / Christian Life

Unless otherwise noted, all Scriptures are taken from the
Holman Christian Standard Bible (HCSB), copyright © 1999,
2000, 2002, 2003 by Holman Bible Publishers. Other trans-
lations used include the New International Version (NIV)
Copyright © 1973, 1978, 1984 International Bible Society.
Used by permission of Zondervan. All rights reserved.
New American Standard Bible (NASB) Copyright © 1960,
1962, 1963, 1968, 1971, 1972, 1973, 1975, 1977, 1995 by
The Lockman Foundation. Used by permission.

Quotations used at the beginning of each chapter are
taken from John Blanchard's *The Complete Gathered Gold*
(Webster, NY: Evangelical Press, 2006).

Printed in the United States
1 2 3 4 5 6 7   12 11 10 09

IN MEMORY OF
RON DUNN AND VANCE HAVNER

Two of the greatest men of God I ever knew. Not a day goes by that I don't miss them. Their influence and impact on my life flavors every page of this book and every sermon I preach. They are such an integral part of my spiritual DNA that I rarely write or speak without quoting them or thinking about them. They were the two great influences and mentors in how I think about ministry, preaching, and the life of surrender. They knew dark valleys and times of desperation, but they never lost their hope in God. Though dead, yet they still speak.

IN HONOR OF
WARREN WIERSBE

God brought Warren into my life a few years before Ron died, primarily through our mutual love for Vance Havner. Warren has become the person most used by God in my life to give me wisdom and insight. He is the most genuinely balanced man I have ever known. To me, he is the balanced blend of spirit and truth, mind and heart. I own every book he's written. God in His grace has allowed me to know Warren as a friend, prayer supporter, and encourager. He is a hero who has become a friend.

TABLE OF CONTENTS

FOREWORD

Feeling that my lungs were about to explode, I kicked desperately against the river's strong current as it drew me inexorably down under and downstream. What had started out as an innocent boyish escapade, diving with my friends off the pier of a bridge, had now resulted in a situation so perilous that I was near panic. Seeing the sunlight through the murky waters above me, I stretched for the water's surface, ultimately bursting through to the top as I simultaneously gasped for the one commodity that had become more precious to me than gold—air!

Desperation is a powerful force. Desperation focuses our attention and energies on the things that count. While none of us enjoys the desperate experience, we revel in the result! Lungs are filled with air! A family is rescued! A body is healed! A nation is saved! A sinner comes to God! A wandering believer whose desolate life has become dry and damaged is driven once again to the fountain of living water into which he plunges with total surrender.

But it is not the dive that brings most of us to a point of desperation these days. We are not given to that kind of risk. It is the drift. Slowly, unwittingly, and with seeming innocence, we drift further and further from fellowship with God. The shores of His grace may seem distant and diminished, but we still have them in view. A turn in the wind, a couple of swift spiritual kicks, and we'll be back where we belong. Or so we think.

A friend of mine once confessed over lunch that he was "broke." When I assured him that I had sufficient resources to cover the meal, he protested, saying that he was not broke financially but spiritually. He then told how he generally met times of spiritual drift with renewed focus on the things of God: a conference here, a convention there, and maybe a pumped up quiet time. "But something strange has happened," my friend continued. "I'm away from God, and this time I can't seem to get back."

My friend likened himself to the proverbial turtle on its back in the middle of a highway. "I can't get back to God," he said, with a note of panic in his voice. His journey had brought him to the shores of desperation. But as you will discover in this book, desperation can be a good thing. It is actually a sign of life—a recognition that things are not what (or where) they should be.

"Desperation always precedes revelation," my now-deceased friend, Manley Beasley, was accustomed to saying. "When you're desperate, God may finally have your attention."

Manley Beasley was only echoing the sentiments of an earlier pilgrim, David, who was well acquainted with desperation. Crouching in the back of the cave of Adullam, surrounded by fugitives with whom he had nothing in common except the desire to escape Saul's wrath, David wrote, "There is no refuge for me; no one cares about me" (Ps. 142:4). But scarcely had those words been penned before David's desperation drove him to this delightful conclusion: "The righteous will gather around me because You deal generously with me" (v. 7).

Desperation can be a good thing if it turns your heart to the Lord.

This is a book for all of us because all of us will become desperate at some point, either from the drift of faithlessness or from the dive of faith. Maybe you're at that point right now. If so, dig in. This book holds gems of truth that will revolutionize your walk with God.

And for those who don't sense desperation just now—read it while you can. You'll be there soon enough.

— **Tom Elliff**

INTRODUCTION

Most of us never seek the Lord until we are forced to. We can easily coast through life and put our spiritual minds in neutral until a crisis comes. Then we turn to God and cry out for help, mercy, intervention, or deliverance. Rather than constantly seeking the Lord, we tend to take Him for granted.

All too often, believers would like to live in the Promised Land without having to face Jericho and the enemies of God. The milk and honey would be great, but we aren't desperate enough to fight for all God has in store for our lives. With the land of promise come battles and blessings. Unfortunately I find myself wanting the blessings but asking God to deliver me from the battles.

Only when our hand is forced do we yield—when our back is to the wall and our fleshly attempts at deliverance are all washed away. We are resistant by nature. We want to be the captain of our own ship, the master of our own destiny. It's in our spiritual DNA, dating all the way back to Adam and Eve.

Sometimes our loving Father has to orchestrate events to get our attention. He loves us, but He will not leave us where He finds us. He waits patiently for our obedience, but if we do not pursue Him, He will pursue us. At various times along the journey, I have been frustrated with life, myself, and even with God. It wasn't until I learned the power of desperation that I was able to move into a new dimension of understanding.

My greatest times with the Lord have not been on the mountaintop. It has been in the battles—personal as well as those that arise in the ministry—where I have found Him ready to meet me. That's because God is attracted to weakness. He hears the cries of the desperate. Over and over again in Scripture, we see God respond to His people when they cry out to Him. He is not an indifferent deity. He is a loving God who allows us to be broken so He can remake us more and more into His image.

Brokenness is not something we sign up for. It's not the elective we choose in order to get an easy grade. But it is a necessity if we are going to be useful to the Master. Like it or not, it is when we are broken that we are made whole. When we are weak, He is strong. In the darkest hour He shines the brightest. In the pit we find the bottom is solid ground.

The idea for this book surprised me. I wasn't thinking about writing a book on this subject, but in a matter of days God gave me the title and the contents. I can look back in my journal and see the day when God gave me the ideas for the chapters you are about to read.

In the following pages, I'm asking you to take a journey with me—the journey of desperation. There is power available for the journey, power in the mere admission of desperation. On these pages we will visit with men and women who met God in their moments of desperation. Maybe you will find a picture of yourself in one of their stories. It is my prayer that God will use this book to stir your heart to want more of Him, to know the fullness of Him, and to appropriate the power that comes to desperate and broken people.

You will also find stories from people I know, people who have been willing to share their journey with me. All give testimony to the increased awareness of God's sufficiency in their times of great desperation.

The men and women God uses are familiar with the power of desperation. Their stories have been handed down from generation to generation. Why? Because we identify with real people facing real issues. We can see ourselves in the text. We can feel the pain of their hearts. We can see the tears in their eyes and hear the cries from their lips.

The power of desperation is something the world cannot comprehend. In a world where strength is lauded, we see that broken people have unexpected power with God. The blessings of the broken and surrendered are immeasurable. Their stories bless us and move us, thousands of years after they are dead and gone.

This is not a self-help book. I am weary of the world's answers, which bring temporary relief but no permanent hope. I pray that you will linger, listen, and embrace these stories.

And I pray that God will use them to touch your heart, encourage your faith, and remind you that He is your source.

May God meet you at the point of your desperation, and may you find encouragement and power to stay on the journey. I invite you to join the fellowship of the desperate—those men and women within the body of Christ who have come to understand the victory in defeat, the power in surrender, and the glory in the cross.

— Michael Catt

CHAPTER 1

THE WAY UP IS DOWN

Genesis 32–35

God cannot bless us until he has us. When we try to keep within us an area that is our own, we try to keep an area of death. Therefore, in love, he claims all. There's no bargaining with him.
— C. S. Lewis

He blessed him there. Jacob then named the place Peniel, "For," he said, "I have seen God face to face, and I have been delivered."
— Genesis 32:29–30

HAVE YOU EVER been backed into a corner? Have you ever felt you had no way out of a situation? What did you do? How did you respond? Did you curse or cry out to God?

Jacob was a master at maneuvering his way out of tight corners. All his life he was known as a schemer, hustler, and supplanter. He was always trying to get the upper hand. You find Jacob constantly trying to wiggle and squirm his way loose from a situation, looking out for number one. But one day, life caught up with him. He realized he was backed into a corner with nowhere to go. God had boxed him in and pinned him down for the count. It brought him to a point of desperation.

I know people who believe that professional wrestling is real. I have a man on my staff who was a professional wrestler before he was saved. He knows better. The matches are planned, rehearsed, and fixed. The outcome is determined before the steroids ever enter the stadium.

I am not a wrestling fan, but I find myself drawn to the first recorded wrestling match in history, located in Genesis 32. Jacob never had a chance; it was a fixed match. There was no doubt who was going to win this one. Jacob wasn't slick enough to slip out of God's hold. God met him and pinned him until he cried out in desperation.

> During the night Jacob got up and took his two wives, his two female slaves, and his 11 sons, and crossed the ford of Jabbok. He took them and brought them across the stream, along with all his possessions.

Jacob was left alone, and a man wrestled with him until daybreak. When the man saw that He could not defeat him, He struck Jacob's hip as they wrestled and dislocated his hip socket. Then He said to Jacob, "Let Me go, for it is daybreak." But Jacob said, "I will not let You go unless You bless me."

"What is your name?" the man asked.

"Jacob!" he replied.

"Your name will no longer be Jacob," He said. "It will be Israel because you have struggled with God and with men and have prevailed."

Then Jacob asked Him, "Please tell me Your name." But He answered, "Why do you ask My name?" And He blessed him there.

Jacob named the place Peniel, "For," he said, "I have seen God face to face, and I have been delivered." The sun shone on him as he passed by Penuel—limping on his hip. That is why, to this day, the Israelites don't eat the thigh muscle that is at the hip socket: because He struck Jacob's hip socket at the thigh muscle. (Gen. 32:22–32)

While we know Jacob as one of the patriarchs, it's important to remember that he was not a perfect man. He was flawed. He was deceptive. From the moment of his birth, he was wrestling to get his way. And what he didn't get by depravity, he got by encouragement. Rebekah, his mother, encouraged him to deceive his own father, Isaac. But ultimately Jacob was to blame for his choices. He chose to deceive his father. He chose to lie. His pattern was lying and deception.

Jacob was an unlikable man. He was like the guy you despised in high school. The bully in the room, the one you never wanted to turn your back on. The boy you wouldn't want your daughter to date. The sad truth is, in many ways, we see too much of ourselves in Jacob. Often when we look in the mirror, we are looking at Jacob.

Some of you are more like Jacob than you want to admit. You can't keep a job, but it's always someone else's fault. Your wife has been insisting that you see a counselor for your anger, but you tell her you can handle it. Your parents have been warning you about the crowd you're hanging out with, but you think they are totally out of touch. Maybe you've listened to sermon after sermon on the victorious life, but you are wallowing in defeat because you keep trying harder instead of trusting completely. Like Jacob, some of us insist on learning everything the hard way.

> **WE SEE TOO MUCH OF OURSELVES IN JACOB. OFTEN WHEN WE LOOK IN THE MIRROR, WE ARE LOOKING AT JACOB.**

Jacob came by his deception naturally. His mother convinced him to dupe his father. Even his conniving uncle Laban gave him a taste of his own medicine. Laban did to Jacob what Jacob had done to his father and brother Esau. He was out-manipulated by Laban and experienced the feeling of being on the receiving end of deception. The philosophy of life in this family was, "The ends justify the means."

Jacob was like a lot of believers today. They've learned the ways of the world. They know how to scheme to their advantage. They sing on Sunday about the cross and then live in deception, manipulation, and lies during the week. What happens on Sunday has very little to do with how they live the rest of their lives. Until . . .

Until they face a crisis. Until the bottom falls out. Until their lives come back to haunt them. Until they meet their match. Until the seeds they sow reap a whirlwind of unbearable consequences. Then, backed into a corner, they become desperate for God.

BETWEEN A ROCK AND A HARD PLACE

As you move from chapter 31 to chapter 32 of Genesis, you find Jacob in a precarious position. Behind him was Laban, so there was no turning back. Ahead was Esau, so what was in front of him wasn't very appealing either. He had cheated his brother out of the birthright. For decades he feared Esau would find him and kill him. As far as he knew, Esau still wanted to kill him.

Jacob was confronted with the possibility that his sin would find him out. What if Esau was bent on revenge and retribution? A guilty conscience doesn't need an accuser, nor will it let you blame someone else. Jacob was without excuse and he knew it. After all he had done to Esau, his conscience was pricked with the thought of his sin and deception. The name "Esau" appears in Genesis 32 a total of nine times. Over and over again Jacob was reminded of the fact that he was headed for a confrontation with his past and his sin. What he didn't know was that God was going to confront him before he ever got to Esau.

It is unbelievable but true that God is the God of Abraham, Isaac, and Jacob. I would have never chosen Jacob. Jacob would not be patriarch material in our eyes. But God sees what we cannot see. He sees Jacob and knows he can become Israel. He sees a twister and supplanter and knows that one day he can learn to trust God in a whole new dimension.

Do you find it hard to love the Jacobs of this world? It's probably because you've convinced yourself that you are better than Jacob. Maybe you think God loves you more than he loves Jacob. But God loves Jacobs—the ones we tend to write off. We give up on them, thinking they aren't worth our time. That's because we've got our eyes on the problem and not the process.

Maybe, just maybe, you are a Jacob reading this book. You're wondering, *After all the lies, deception, and conniving, can God ever use me? Why would God want to use me? Is there hope for me?*

I have a friend who said of another brother in Christ who has failed multiple times, "I want to be the one person he can turn to and know he is loved unconditionally. I don't approve of what he's done. I don't applaud it. But someone has to love him, and it might as well be me."

Maybe you are a Jacob, or you know a Jacob. Jacob is the one who says he wants to serve God but tries to do it in his flesh. The one who uses carnal methods and strategies in hopes of attaining the blessings and promises of God. The one who sees life as one extended negotiation process, constantly looking for loopholes in lordship, obedience, and holiness.

Jacob's life is the biography of a man in conflict between his flesh and the Spirit. We see his depravity against the backdrop of God's desire to use him. Theodore Epp wrote, "Believers [grow] weary of the conflict between the flesh and the Spirit, and some wonder when there will no longer be the inner struggle. As long as we are in these earthly bodies, there will be the struggle of our two natures. As we walk with God we will learn what to expect of the old nature and how to cope with it, but the conflict will always be there. . . . As God worked with Jacob, little by little, He was able to instill in his heart the realization that the old nature is totally depraved and nothing good can be expected of it."[1]

At the end of his life, Jacob gave a brief biographical sketch to Pharaoh: "My pilgrimage has lasted 130 years. My years have been few and hard, and they have not surpassed the years of my fathers during their pilgrimages" (Gen. 47:9). Scripture interprets the word "hard" in a number of ways. It is translated: evil, distress, adversity, affliction, calamity, mischief, trouble, wretchedness, and wickedness. It reminds us that sin is extremely destructive.

In other words, in spite of the fact that God redeemed his later days and renamed him, Jacob viewed his life as a wasted life. He had spent a great deal of energy and time running from God, fighting God, resisting the Lord, and ripping people off.

The good news is that he didn't play the blame game. He didn't point a finger at his mother and say, "She taught me to be this way." He didn't say, "If you knew Laban like I knew Laban . . ."

We will never be desperate for God if we blame our environment, our education or lack thereof, our surroundings, our parents, or our circumstances. I've visited prisons and heard inmates blame the system, the man, or their absentee father. The reality is this: we do make choices. Two people can be in identical situations; one turns to God while the other shakes his fist at God. One has a pity party, and the other praises God in spite of it all.

We will never be desperate until we face our own depravity. Sin deceives us into thinking we can negotiate with God. It deludes us into believing that we can get better in our flesh. It destroys us by telling us we can get to heaven but avoid a face-to-face encounter with the Christ who demands our whole life surrendered to Him.

THE POINT OF DESPERATION

Bringing a person to the point of desperation is a process. We want instant change, but sometimes it takes time to get the junk out of our lives. God works with us where we are. He refines, rebukes, and reveals as He moves us toward righteousness and personal revival.

In Jacob's dream, given to him while on the run from his murder-minded brother, God made a promise: "Look, I am with you and will watch over you wherever you go. I will bring you back to this land, for I will not leave you until I have done what

I have promised you" (Gen. 28:15). Jacob woke up from the dream and realized, "God was in this place!"

God is patient. He will pursue us like the hound of heaven because He longs to catch us, wrestle us to the ground, and bring us to a blessing. The blessing can't come without the wrestling. If there is no willingness to yield, there will never be willingness for God to rule.

God saw something in Jacob that we wouldn't see with a casual glance. Here was a man we would have given up on long ago, but God didn't give up on Jacob. Why? He wanted Jacob to surrender so he could become something by the power of God—something he could never become on his own.

THE BLESSING CAN'T COME WITHOUT THE WRESTLING. IF THERE IS NO WILLINGNESS TO YIELD, THERE WILL NEVER BE WILLINGNESS FOR GOD TO RULE.

Jacob's wrestling match in Genesis 32 was a defining moment in his life. Jacob, the supplanter, now had power with God. The deceiver now realized his strength through Jehovah. Where he once tried to prevail in his own strength, Jacob now found God's power to prevail in a new way. He was knocked down so he could one day stand up in victory.

In Genesis 35, Jacob was once again at Bethel, where God renewed the promise to Jacob by changing his name to Israel. "Your name is Jacob; you will no longer be named Jacob, but Israel will be your name. . . . The land that I gave to Abraham and Isaac I will give to you. And I will give the land to your descendants after you" (vv. 10, 12). God fulfilled His promise. Jacob lived out a blessed life, but it wasn't without struggle.

I recently pulled down an old copy of A. W. Tozer's classic *The Knowledge of the Holy*. In the preface of that book I found these words: "Modern Christianity is simply not producing the kind of Christian who can appreciate or experience the life in the Spirit. . . . The only way to recoup our spiritual losses is to go back to the cause of them and make such corrections as the truth warrants. The decline of the knowledge of the holy has brought on our troubles."[2]

Why did Jacob fall prey to deceit? He didn't have a proper view of God, a proper "knowledge of the holy." He wanted God's will, his way. It never works like that. Only when we come to the end of ourselves will we ever find the beginning of a fresh touch from God. We are so busy with our schemes, dreams, and plans that we have little time for intimacy, holiness, and—yes— desperation. Thus, God has to orchestrate events where He can get us alone and wrestle our stubborn will to the ground.

Jacob, like many of us, knew the promise of the blessing, but he couldn't see how God was going to do it. He was impatient with God's timetable. He must have been convinced the promise was conditional based on something he could do, rather than unconditional based on the wisdom, grace, and love of God.

But Jacob didn't get it, and sometimes neither do we. The only way he could see things working out was if he got involved in the process and was proactive. So he stole the birthright, he lied, he manipulated, until—faced with the prospect of losing it all—he met God.

Don't think that we all embrace the idea of "knowing God." Jacob didn't. He was willing to send all he had ahead to appease his angry brother Esau. As Gene Getz says, Jacob was going to "test the waters." He didn't really care what happened to everyone else as long as he could save his own hide. For the longest time, Jacob just didn't get it. He thought he could control his family, his life, and his future. As one writer said, "Striving and resisting become a survival tactic."[3]

God is bound by His nature to finish the work He has started in us. Jacob had to come face-to-face with himself and his deceptive patterns. God could not leave Jacob where He found him. Salvation must result in sanctification. If we are ever going to be used of God, to see life in a new light, to walk in a new dimension of our faith, we must be pinned to the mat. We must yield, repent, and surrender.

WHERE THE PAST GOES TO DIE

The flesh dies hard. Jacob, on his way back to meet Esau, fell back into his old thought patterns. His actions reveal his inability to trust God with his life. Still unable to completely release himself to the Lord, he tried to make promises of elaborate gifts to appease Esau. For Jacob, bribery was easier than humility and brokenness.

But God knew how to get Jacob's attention. When God wrestles with us, He has a twofold purpose: to get us to admit our deception and to reveal what we can be when we are desperate for Him as our source of sufficiency. Jacob named the place of wrestling "Peniel," which means "the face of God."

I often heard Manley Beasley say, "A glimpse of Jesus will save you, but to gaze at Him will sanctify you."

This night brought significant change to the once crafty twister. He was unsure if any of his plans would work. He didn't know what tomorrow would bring. He was alone and afraid. But he crossed the ford of the Jabbok. Crossing over the river is essential if we are ever going to move beyond ourselves. Jacob was not only crossing over; he was moving in a new direction. He was leaving the old behind—Laban, his name, his past. He was entering into a new phase in his experience with God.

Jacob looked at his past, and he was ashamed. He looked at his future—at the thought of facing Esau—and he was afraid. It's possible his mind was flooded with family stories of God's faithfulness to his grandfather, Abraham. He knew they were true for Abraham but wasn't sure the same would be true for himself. Thus, in spite of all that God had done to preserve Jacob's life, to bless him, and to reveal Himself to him, Jacob was still far short of where he should have been in his walk with Jehovah.

WHEN A MAN OR WOMAN GETS DESPERATE FOR GOD, THEY CAN GET THROUGH TO GOD.

It is true that God often works in a slow manner, refining and pruning us. But there are times when God deals with us suddenly and decisively. This is what happened to Jacob. The Holy Spirit can do more to change your life in five minutes than you or I can imagine. Jacob's encounter with the living God was life-changing. He learned more that night than he had learned his entire life.

Scripture says that "a man wrestled with him until daybreak" (Gen. 32:24). This wasn't a fight that was finished in a few minutes. It was an exhausting, stressful, crisis experience. He didn't know if he would live or die. It was hand-to-hand combat.

Finally as the day began to break, Jacob tried to discover the name of the wrestler. The Angel of the Lord turned the tables on Jacob and asked, "What is your name?" Gene Getz brilliantly describes this moment: "When the stranger asked Jacob's name, Jacob must have released his grip and fallen limp at the stranger's feet, whispering his own name in shame. The physical battle was over—and so was the spiritual battle that was far more important than the wrestling match. For most of his life, Jacob had promoted his own agenda. He was self-centered and self-driven. He was used to making his own way in life, deceiving when necessary. He relied on his own strength—both psychologically and physically. . . . It was during this moment of weakness, while Jacob was exerting all the human strength he could muster, that God brought him to his knees and changed his name."[4]

When a man or woman gets desperate for God, they can get through to God. He is attracted to weakness. Our strengths are no help to Him. Our weakness is where He can prove Himself to be our source of sufficiency. Notice in Genesis 32:29, "And He blessed him there." He blessed Jacob at the point of his surrender and abandonment. He blessed him in ways he could have never been blessed otherwise.

If Jacob had been given a vote, he would have never chosen to meet the Angel of the Lord. Yet it was a defining moment in his life. It forever changed him. He was struck in the thigh and walked with a limp the rest of his life. Whatever others might have thought of his limp, Jacob knew it to be a constant reminder of God's victory over him. When he limped along, his body would move up and then move down. Jacob learned in his desperate situation that the way up is down.

Maybe you are feeling alone. Maybe you are immersed in a time of darkness in your life. Could it be your sin is catching up with you? Are you tired of running? I've got good news for you. God is on the verge of getting you alone with Him so He can get the "you" out of you and fill you with Himself. The sooner you acknowledge who you are and what you are, the sooner you'll find He has a blessing for you. Your surrender will become His victory . . . in you and through you.

The light at the end of your darkness is a wrestling match where God can change your name, transform you more and more into His image, and then mold you into a witness of His amazing grace.

THE SUFFICIENCY AND SUPPLY OF GOD IN THE WILDERNESS

Deuteronomy 8

The grace, the groans and the glory are all part of the eternal purpose. Where there is no groaning, there is no growing now, nor glory to come.
— Vance Havner

Remember that the Lord your God led you on the entire journey these 40 years in the wilderness, so that He might humble you and test you to know what was in your heart, whether or not you would keep His commands.
— Deuteronomy 8:2

19

IF YOU'VE LIVED VERY LONG, you've experienced the wilderness. There's been a time in your life when you've wandered in the desert, trying to figure out why the promises of God have not come true in your life. The wilderness experience of Israel is an accurate historical experience with great spiritual lessons. Their wandering was the result of unbelief because they refused to believe all the promises of God. The majority never tasted of the land of milk and honey.

Will you live and die in the wilderness, or will you so desire what God wants for your life that you will push through any obstacles, any doubt, any fear, and step out in faith? I'm not talking about postmodern America where we are bombarded with the prosperity, feel-good, "what's in it for me" distortion of the gospel. We live in a time when every religious channel seems to be filled with messages about power, success, fame, and fortune. Leadership is emphasized more than lordship. Being a dynamic person is treated as being more significant than daily discipleship. The big "I" is center stage while God takes the backseat.

In fact, God is our servant in this kind of theology and thinking. If you follow God, you can demand that sickness be removed, pain be eliminated, and suffering be extinguished. In the "health and wealth" gospel, there's no need for desperation—it's all yours for the taking. I might be tempted to believe this stuff myself if I hadn't read my Bible.

There's no room in Americanized Christianity for books on pain, disease, suffering, famine, tears, trials, and tribulations. The late Ron Dunn wrote one of the finest and soundest theological books on the subject of healing ever written, entitled *Will God Heal Me?* The book has never sold as well as it should simply because Ron understood that Scripture does not guarantee healing in all situations, nor does it teach that healing is in the atonement. This causes problems for people who want books to tell them what they want to hear, not what they *need* to hear. Do a Web search on brokenness or the wilderness, and you won't discover many sites that deal with these topics from a spiritual perspective.

In my opinion, many books today in "Christian" literature hardly have a balanced view of life. Most read like a fairy tale to anyone who has dealt with the realities of our existence. The lighter the gospel, the better the sales. The more cotton candy theology, the more cash in the pocket of the author. These writers are selling books that promise a life free from burdensome experiences. As I scan the bookshelves of the average Christian bookstore, I find shelf after shelf of "me first" books. The commentaries, if there are any, are stuck in the back corner because they don't sell. What sells today are books with titles like:

- *Your Best Life Now*
- *Step into Divine Destiny*
- *You're All That*
- *8 Steps to Create the Life You Want*
- *21 Days to Your Spiritual Makeover*
- *Claim Your Victory Today*
- *Total Life Prosperity*
- *Look Great, Feel Great*

In truth, these books are not theologically honest. They are best sellers but often fall short of the truths found in Scripture. They lean on pop psychology and Oprah's opinions, splatter in a few Scriptures, and call it biblical teaching. They use humor but rarely talk about holiness. These books use the same philosophy as those found in the leadership, business, and money sections of secular bookstores. Check out these titles and see if you see any similarities:

- *Secrets of the Millionaire Mind: Mastering the Inner Game of Wealth*
- *Trump University Wealth Building 101*
- *The Road to Wealth*
- *The Science of Getting Rich*
- *Success Is Not an Accident: Change Your Choices, Change Your Life*
- *The Seven Spiritual Laws of Success*
- *The Science of Success*

You won't find many books on the refiner's fire, the wilderness, dangers, toils, and snares. Today's authors often try to deal with life from the lite side. They make cotton-candy promises. Cotton candy is great, but it's really just fancied-up sugar. Once you get over the high, you are back to reality. In this instant solution to problems approach, the thought of God taking forty years to work something in us—and out of us—is frightening.

WILDERNESS ROADS

The dictionary defines "wilderness" as a tract or region that is uncultivated, uninhabited by human beings, an area essentially undisturbed by human activity together with its naturally developed life community. The wilderness is a wild region or pathless area or remote space. There are nearly three hundred references to the wilderness in the Old and New Testaments. It was often a place of wandering, but there was always a purpose to it. The children of Israel, for example, wandered forty years in the wilderness for failing to obey God, but He taught them some valuable truths along the way.

While there is little in the way of books about failure, most of the personalities in Scripture that God viewed as worthy of mentioning went through a time of testing or failure. Study the Bible and you'll find that every person God uses has gone through adversity. Men and women of whom the world is not worthy are rarely recognized by the secular world. In the eyes of many, Noah, Moses, Job, and the prophets would be considered failures. They never achieved according to the world's standards. But what they learned in their times of testing qualified them to be honored in the hall of faith in the book of Hebrews.

We would do well to note that most of them did not have what our twenty-first-century Christianity calls a "blessed" life. I imagine Job's testimony would have been "serving God when there's nothing left." Moses' testimony would have been "how to go from the palace to the desert in one fateful decision." Noah would have said, "Don't build a boat where there's no water, unless you are willing to be the brunt of the world's jokes."

These and countless others suffered, struggled, and sacri-ficed. They went through deep, dark valleys of persecution and difficulty. They dealt with nearly impossible family situ-ations and were rejected by their own. They were laughed at and rebelled against, yet through it all they kept their eyes on the author and perfecter of their faith. These believers knew they were "in process." They didn't allow the event to overshadow the journey. The pruning had a purpose, and the wilderness did what nothing else could do.

You can't honestly read your Bible and come to the same conclusions these "health and wealth" preachers do. They are wrong in their hermeneutics and self-centered in their interpre-tations. They teach strange doctrines, using smoke and mirrors. They promise what they can't produce.

When things don't work out perfectly, and when we come to a place of desperation, we can conclude one of three things: 1) We can believe that God created the heavens and the earth and now just sits back and watches us. We are simply caught in a cause-and-effect sequence. 2) We can believe that God is not really sovereign and that He has limited power or no control over our circumstances. 3) We can conclude that God is sov-ereign and nothing happens in our lives unless He allows it or orchestrates it.

I don't know one soul who would choose the wilderness. Jeremiah, however, said it was a place where the people found grace. Isaiah referred to a time when the wilderness would rejoice. John the Baptist preached good news in the wilderness. Jesus was sustained even in His time of temptation in the wilderness.

The wilderness can be a transforming place. Could it be said that the wilderness is what you make it? For those who disobeyed God and did not take Him at His word, it was a place of discipline and death. For others, it was a place of learning to trust God. The people of God complained for hundreds of years about their Egyptian bondage. When God finally set them free and they were led out by Moses, some of them found every means possible to undermine God's work, God's man, and God's process. The path of life is not *around* the wilderness but *through* it. It's how you respond to the wilderness that determines whether you get to the other side, the Promised Land of victory.

Robert Bailey, in his book *The Wilderness Experience*, writes, "The wilderness is an experience of contrasts. It is an unsettled, barren, perilous area, but it is also a place where God is! It is a difficult, lonely, unnerving site, but it is also a place where God dwells! It is a draining, exhausting, discouraging situation, but it is also a place where God heals and strengthens! It is a removed, desolate, debilitating condition, but it is also a place where God moves and loves!"[1]

BY WAY OF THE WILDERNESS

Deuteronomy 8 tells us that God led the children of Israel in the wilderness. When they blew it and didn't obey God, He didn't dump them in the wilderness or abandon them in the desert. He led them every step of the way. He used the wilderness to teach them about themselves and about His faithfulness.

If you go to the New Testament, you find the Spirit led Jesus into the wilderness to be tempted. If the people of God were led into the wilderness and the Lord Himself was led into the wilderness, what would ever make us conclude that we could avoid a wilderness experience? Why would we think for one minute we might be immune from such a test?

The wilderness always has a purpose. God always has a plan. He takes these times to prune us, to purge us of that which is unnecessary, and to prepare us for the next step in our faith journey. Even a casual study of Scripture would reveal the Bible knows nothing of a life without struggles. These struggles are intended to drive us to God. They are used by God to teach us, lead us, and prepare us for what He has ahead for us.

> Remember that the Lord your God led you on the entire journey these 40 years in the wilderness, so that He might humble you and test you to know what was in your heart, whether or not you would keep His commands. He humbled you by letting you go hungry; then He gave you manna to eat, which you and your fathers had not known, so that you might learn that man does not live on bread alone but on every word that comes from the mouth of the Lord. Your clothing did not wear out, and your feet did not swell these 40 years. Keep in mind that the Lord your God has been disciplining you just as a man disciplines his son. So keep the commands of the Lord your God by walking in His ways and by fearing Him. (Deut. 8:2–6)

Words in this passage that describe humility leap out to me. The wilderness is used by God to humble us. James McCosh writes, "True humility is a Christian grace and one of the fruits of the Spirit originating in a deep consciousness of sin past and present, leading us to discover our nothingness in the view of God, our insufficiency for anything that is good, and prompting us, as we feel our infirmities, to strive after higher and yet higher attainments."[2] God doesn't put us in the wilderness to destroy us but to develop us.

Humility doesn't come naturally to us. We are not humble by nature, so God has to break us of our pride. Swallowing our pride is not something we do willingly, but it seldom results in indigestion. In reality, swallowing our pride leads us to a new dimension of power in our Christian life. God is attracted to desperation and weakness. He looks for the broken so He can bless them. William Bridge writes, "If you lay yourself at Christ's feet, He will take you into His arms."[3] Humility is the ability to see ourselves as God sees us.

GOD DOESN'T PUT US IN THE WILDERNESS TO DESTROY US BUT TO DEVELOP US.

In his commentary on this passage, Warren Wiersbe writes, "The three essentials for Israel's conquest and enjoyment of the Promised Land were: listening to God's Word, remembering it, and obeying it. They are still the essentials for a successful and satisfying Christian life today. As we walk through this world, we can't succeed without God's guidance, protection, and provision, and it also helps to have a good memory. Four times in these chapters Moses commands us to remember . . . and four more times he admonishes us to forget not."[4] It's what we should remember when we keep forgetting that keeps us in the wilderness longer than the original plan.

The history of Israel is not a perfect history recorded by a politically correct theologian. God reveals His people in all their inconsistencies and failures. When Moses wrote these words, he was giving us a recap of the checkered past of the people of God. At times they cried out to God for deliverance. At other times they complained to God and longed to return to Egypt. The one truth I draw from this text is that God puts us in the wilderness until we want the Promised Land enough to fight for it. Listening to, remembering, and obeying the Word of God is essential if we are going to learn all He intends for us to learn in the wilderness.

GOD PUTS US IN THE WILDERNESS UNTIL WE WANT THE PROMISED LAND ENOUGH TO FIGHT FOR IT.

God did not abandon His people. He made daily provisions for them and protected them from their enemies. The wilderness was long and hard, but it didn't have to be lonely.

It would help some of us in our journey to see that God leads us in the wilderness. What we will not embrace by faith and obedience to His Word, we unfortunately must often learn through painful experiences. Some of us stumble into the wilderness because we take our eyes off the Lord, while others find themselves in the wilderness because they've been impacted by the decisions of others. Whatever the reason, God is with us in the wilderness. The question is: Are we with God in the process?

It is not God who forgets, it's us. The people of Israel were reminded, "Be careful that you don't forget the Lord your God." When we forget God's goodness and grace and our need for total dependence, He sometimes leads us into the wilderness to remind us we are nothing without Him. When life is going our way, we tend to forget. When we take God's blessings for granted, we tend to forget. When we assume we can make the journey on our own, we tend to forget it is God who provides for us and sustains us. Familiarity breeds contempt. Abundance of blessings can, in fact, take the edge off our pursuit of God. He will not allow us to live with a "give me my daily bread only" mentality. He expects more from us. He's not here to serve us; we are here to surrender to Him.

Because of their lack of faith, their rebellion, and their inconsistencies, the people were in the wilderness. Although God provided manna from heaven, it was a far cry from the land flowing with milk and honey. Too many are content in the wilderness, wandering but not walking in victory, sustained but not enriched, filled with manna but not full of all that God desires. To resist the will of God and ignore His Word will lead you into a barren experience where you *exist* but you don't necessarily *abound* in the blessings that could be yours.

O LET ME NE'ER FORGET

The children of Israel were confined to the wilderness for forty years, wandering like bedouins. The journey to the land of promise should have taken eleven days, but it took them forty years. They had a committee meeting and decided they knew better than God, and it cost an entire generation. They came to Kadesh-Barnea and refused to obey God's Word and His will. They weren't willing to trust God and move forward by faith. They rejected the promises and plan of God. Of the men, all but two died in the wilderness. Rather than spending those forty years tasting and seeing that the Lord is good, they spent every day going to funerals until the unfaithful and disobedient died off.

In his sermon "Perils of the Good Life," Stuart Briscoe talks about the "perils of self-interest, self-indulgence, and self-sufficiency." He goes on to say, "Prosperity can lead to pride. Pride leads to a sense of power. Power is blind to the One who provides."[5] Isn't that what always happens? Alumni forget that the coach they want to fire was coach of the year just two years ago. Kids forget the sacrifices their parents have made. Staff members leave a church and then begin to talk negatively about it. They forget this was the church that paid their salary, their health insurance, and their benefits the whole time they were employed there.

When we forget, we lose our sense of wonder and gratitude. Ron Dunn used to say the epitaph of these people could have been, "They died in the wilderness." They never got all God had for them. They never knew the joy of walking in victory. They were saved but defeated, forgiven but not filled. It took Israel forty years to learn to walk through God's open doors of opportunity, to fight for the land God had given them.

God used the wilderness to teach them valuable lessons. He knocked off the rough edges, pruned the dead branches, and taught them to trust. They were still led by God, by the pillar of fire and cloud, but they weren't walking in all God had for them. They were fed but not filled. They were sustained but not satisfied. Why? No desperation. No willingness to go after God whatever the cost. They wanted it easy.

Abraham Poljak, a Jew who escaped from Nazi Germany in World War II, said, "I thank God for all the strokes with which I was driven from darkness into light. It is better that we arrive beaten and bleeding at the glorious goal than that we decay happily and contented in darkness. As long as things were right with us, we did not know anything of God and the salvation of our souls."

The wilderness can indeed be a productive time. Sufferings have their purpose. They drive us to desperation and prayer. Remember Paul's thorn in the flesh? It was a messenger of Satan but also a gift of God's grace. God doesn't allow tough times so that He can be relieved of responsibility. He allows them to reveal to us His will. In Deuteronomy 6:23 we read, "But he brought us from there in order to lead us in and give us the land that He swore to our fathers." God did not abandon them, nor does He abandon us.

DON'T MAKE A WASTELAND OUT OF A WILDERNESS

The wilderness is never wasted time. God uses the wilderness as a learning lab. The people of Israel learned to trust God in the wilderness for their daily bread and for their protection. They also had hundreds of thousands of graves to visibly remind them of the consequences that resulted from not trusting God. The rebellion and lack of faith of those who had gone before them resulted in never seeing the Promised Land. What began as a glorious possibility in the deliverance from Egypt did not translate into a glorious life in the land God had promised them.

Isn't that true of many believers? They are delivered from sin, but somehow they are never delivered from self. They are set free from their past, but they live in failure and defeat in their present. They stop seeking. They settle, get comfortable, and lose their passion and purpose. They become "good" Christians with little impact for the kingdom. Wandering in circles, they mindlessly move from home to school, to career, to retirement, to glory, but

> **WHAT YOU DO AND HOW YOU RESPOND IN THE WILDERNESS DETERMINES WHICH SIDE OF THE RIVER YOU DIE ON.**

they never make a real difference. They are buried and soon forgotten because they left nothing worth remembering, not by God's standards.

The wilderness is a place and time ordained by God. It's also a time when you can make a choice: I'm going to live through this and thrive in the wilderness, or I'm going to curl up in the fetal position and just wait to die. What you do and how you respond in the wilderness determines which side of the river you die on. Every great saint in Christian history has gone through a wilderness experience. Read the biographies of our heroes, and you'll find all of them walked through the desert. Some dealt with depression, others with difficult churches or people. Some had terrible family situations. But all of them learned to see God and trust Him as He led them in and through the wilderness, where they came to the end of self-will and self-sufficiency.

If we are not in tune with God and find ourselves in a wilderness experience, we will be ignorant of what He is trying to do. We could stubbornly refuse to submit to His will. If we are thick-headed, slow to learn, or rebellious, the wilderness could take a long time.

Ruth Bell Graham once enumerated four things that make trials easier: "One, it helps when I know who is in control. Two, it helps when I know I'm not alone in my suffering. Three, it helps when I know the purpose of God is behind it. Four, it helps because I become more compassionate with and understanding of others."[6]

I know in my own experience that I'm more sympathetic with ministers who are going through difficult times because of the difficult times I've experienced. In talking with many pastors, I often find them overwhelmed with discouragement, traveling the road of despair and defeat. I am aware of how difficult it really is to walk in the wilderness according to God's leading and to believe that He will deliver you in His time.

Every time you see a person used by God, you see someone who has had to unlearn self and learn Christ. Moses was an expert on the wilderness experience. He tried to do God's will his own way, and it resulted in being banished to the back side of the desert for forty years. In those forty years the great leader learned to be led. He earned a B.N. (Be Nothing) degree in the seminary of suffering and sheepherding. Faith works best when there is no natural hope. God speaks best when all other voices are silenced. The great man of faith George Mueller once said, "Remember it is the very time for faith to work when sight ceases. The greater the difficulty, the easier for faith; as long as there remains certain natural prospects, faith does not get on as easily."

FULL DISCLOSURE

The hardest part of the wilderness experience is seeing what's really in our hearts. God removes the façades. He cares nothing about how great our peers say we are. He knows the truth, and He reveals it to us. He uses the dust and desert to expose our hearts and our motives. "Remember that the LORD your God led you on the entire journey these 40 years in the wilderness, so that He might humble you and test you *to know what was in your heart*, whether or not you would keep His commands" (Deut. 8:2, italics added).

God knows my heart is deceitful and wicked. In the movie *Fireproof*, there is a line that says we have to *lead* our hearts. We can't trust our feelings. We can feel good about ourselves when really we are displeasing in God's sight. God sometimes has to engineer failure to knock the props out from under us and reveal our hidden weaknesses and flaws that keep us from His divine design. In reality, our strengths are no help to God, and our weaknesses are no hindrance to Him.

I remember one of my better moments when I was mowing the lawn and the lawn mower quit. I checked the plug, checked the gas, and then did what any man of God would do—I started kicking the lawn mower and calling it names. What was happening? My lawn mower was revealing my true self. I got angry at an inanimate object. Something designed to cut grass actually cut me down to size. I realized how easily I could preach about Christ on Sunday and then kick and yell at a lawn mower on Monday. The lawn mower wasn't the problem; it just revealed the problem of my heart.

The Bible warns us about the diseased state of our hearts:

> Before I was afflicted I went astray, but now
> I keep Your word. . . . It was good for me to
> be afflicted so that I could learn Your statutes.
> (Ps. 119:67, 71)

> The heart is more deceitful than anything else
> and desperately sick—who can understand it?
> (Jer. 17:9)

> For I know that nothing good lives in me, that
> is, in my flesh. (Rom. 7:18)

The unguarded moments often reveal our hearts. The unexamined life can lead to spiritual disaster. It's better that the Lord reveals to us our heart and we learn to deal with it, than that we fail to deal with it and let sin's consequences expose it.

God is not looking for you to rededicate your life. You can't rededicate what hasn't been dedicated. He is looking for admission, confession, surrender, and obedience. What He wants is not rededication of our flesh to be better. He wants repentance from the sin that so easily besets us. We should ask God to put a thorn in every pleasure and a worm in every desire that would prevent us from being wholly committed to the lordship of Christ.

SCHOOL'S IN SESSION

What does God want you to learn in the wilderness? "He humbled you by letting you go hungry; then He gave you manna to eat, which you and your fathers had not known, *so that you might learn that man does not live on bread alone, but on every word that comes from the mouth of the Lord*" (Deut. 8:3, italics added). We are placed in the wilderness to learn to feast at the Lord's table and to trust Him for our daily bread. The Word of God is described as milk, meat, bread, and honey. But if we don't stay in the Word, we find ourselves eating the junk food of this world.

> **COULD IT BE THAT GOD DIVINELY DESIGNS DESERT TIMES TO TAKE US TO THE PLACE OF DESPERATION?**

God makes you hungry so He can feed you. He supplies His people with spiritual food that satisfies. Whatever your wilderness, God has a provision. He is working to make you understand the source of life. Your wilderness may be:

- Failing resources
- Diminishing health
- Insignificant worries
- Bad church experience
- Declining business
- Faltering marriage
- Wayward child
- Broken spirit

Whatever form it takes, God ordains the wilderness so we'll learn to lean on Him. At first the Promised Land didn't mean enough to the Israelites to fight for it, but after forty years in the wilderness, they were ready to fight for that milk and honey. God gets us to the point where we'll become desperate enough to get on our knees and get in the Word.

Patrick, the patron saint of Ireland, wrote:

> The power of God to guide me,
> The might of God to uphold me,
> The wisdom of God to teach me,
> The eye of God to watch over me,
> The ear of God to hear me,
> The Word of God to speak to me,
> The hand of God to protect me,
> The way of God to lie before me,
> The shield of God to shelter me,
> The hosts of God to defend me.
> Christ with me, Christ before me,

> Christ beneath me, Christ above me,
> Christ at my right, Christ at my left,
> Christ in breadth, Christ in length,
> Christ in height, Christ in the heart.

God may have you at a rock with no water, a desert with no bread, and a river with no bridge. He hasn't led you there to destroy you but to ultimately bless you with a new revelation of Himself. If you are there, learn the lessons, let God humble you, and don't fall into the trap of complaining about where you are. Christ has led you there to teach you things you would never learn otherwise. Focus on the unchanging Christ whose love is inexhaustible and whose arm never grows tired.

I love Psalm 63, which deals with a wilderness time in David's life. It was not a time of his own choosing. He wasn't there because of sin or unbelief. He was there because of the sinfulness of his son Absalom. The background for this psalm is found in 1 Samuel 15–19. David longed to get back home to Jerusalem. His heart was heavy. C. H. Spurgeon gave great insight into this psalm (as always) when he wrote, "David didn't leave off singing because he was in the wilderness, neither did he in slovenly idleness go on repeating Psalms intended for other occasions; but he carefully made his worship suitable to his circumstances and presented to God his wilderness hymn when he was in a wilderness. There was no desert in his heart, although there was desert around him."

This psalm is a good one to remember when you don't feel like singing, when your back's against the wall, or when you're at the end of your rope. The wilderness was a picture of David's heart. He was struggling, restless, and sleepless, but he found the Lord there.

"God, You are my God; I eagerly seek You. I thirst for You; my body faints for You in a land that is dry, desolate, and without water" (Ps. 63:1). If you read this psalm carefully, you will notice how often David used personal pronouns. He was affirming and declaring his faith in Jehovah in spite of circumstances. What he learned in the sanctuary, he was now applying in the wilderness. His faith was not theoretical but personal. "O God, You are—right now, in this difficult moment—my God, my one and only hope." He was exiled from the throne but not from the One who reigns from the throne of heaven.

God is looking for saints who thirst for Him and yearn for Him. God meets people at springs of refreshing when they thirst for Him. God feeds us with manna from above when we hunger for Him.

> I long and yearn for the courts of the LORD;
> my heart and flesh cry out for the living God.
> (Ps. 84:2)

> I spread out my hands to You; I am like parched
> land before You. (Ps. 143:6)

> Blessed are those who hunger and thirst for
> righteousness, because they will be filled.
> (Matt. 5:6)

Could it be that God divinely designs desert times to take us to the place of desperation? Is God allowing or orchestrating something in your life right now so that you may come to the point of relying on Him completely? As you read Psalm 63 and apply it to your situation, you will see how David acknowledged God's faithfulness in the past; he had not forgotten God. He also affirmed God's faithfulness in the present; God had not forgotten him. In other words, his soul was following hard after God. He was not sitting in the dust complaining. He was in the wilderness confessing that God's right hand was holding him up and sustaining him. David is a reminder to all of us to seek God in our desert experiences.

God knows where you are. He is in total control of the situation. He is inviting you to seek Him with all your heart, to lean on Him and allow Him to sustain you. He hasn't led you there to destroy you but to develop you into the image of His Son. Don't waste your sorrows. Turn your wandering into wonder, your pain into praise, your dust into delight, your fears into faith. Keep marching forward because the Promised Land is in sight. In the words of Thomas Merton:

> My Lord God,
> I have no idea where I am going.
> I do not see the road ahead of me.
> I cannot know for certain
> where it will end.
> Nor do I really know myself,
> and the fact that I think

that I am following your will
does not mean that I am actually doing so.

But I believe that the desire to please you
does in fact please you.
And I hope that I have that desire
in all that I am doing.
I hope that I will never do anything
apart from that desire.
And I know that if I do this
you will lead me by the right road
though I may know nothing about it.

Therefore will I trust you always
though I may seem to be lost
and in the shadow of death.
I will not fear, for you are with me,
and will never leave me
to face my perils alone.[7]

CHAPTER 3

FILL MY CUP, LORD

2 Kings 4:1–7

We will never crave to be filled until we are convinced that we are empty.
—John Blanchard

I pray that you, being rooted and firmly established in love, may be able to comprehend with all the saints what is the breadth and width, height and depth, and to know the Messiah's love that surpasses knowledge, so you may be filled with all the fullness of God.
—Ephesians 3:17–19

WHEN I WAS GROWING UP, The Guess Who had a popular Top-40 song entitled "Hang On to Your Life." I meet a lot of people who are hanging on. They are barely getting by, living paycheck-to-paycheck or crisis-to-crisis. Difficult times abound on every corner.

Jill Briscoe has written an excellent book called A *Little Pot of Oil.* At the beginning of the book she writes, "All of us, no matter what age we are, know what it feels like to run out of something or someone at some time for some reason. But here is one thing you never need to run out of, and that is God."[1]

As I write these words, a pastor friend and his wife are going through a difficult time. She is receiving treatments for cancer. Her sister died several years ago from cancer, so you can imagine the anxiety that confronts them on a daily basis.

I've watched these friends survive and thrive in terrible times. They've led at least two churches where the lay leadership was so carnal they didn't want to see lives changed and people saved. This friend was once the pastor of a very large and prestigious church. Today he pastors in a small community of less than five thousand, and most of his friends have forgotten him. But he is doing his greatest work for God. He is having incredible influence in the community. They are seeing lost adults come to Christ, and the church is in an expansion program.

It has not been without battles, however. People have been fighting him from day one. At times I know he's felt alone, abandoned, forgotten, and unappreciated. Yet he labors on, and God is beginning to show him fruit from his labors.

When he called me to tell me about his wife's cancer diagnosis, I heard the desperation in his voice. His sobbing could be felt hundreds of miles away. His pain and their fears touched our hearts. They are praying, desperate for God to work and to bring healing to her body. God hears their cries.

Our churches and communities are filled with desperate, hurting people. They are at the end of their rope. It may be the result of a doctor's report, a failed business, the death of a loved one, or a troubled marriage. Someone needs to bring hope and healing oil into their lives.

I realize I'm writing a book that will not be consumed by the masses. The masses never admit they are in trouble. They would rather look good at all costs than admit how desperate they really are. I talked to someone recently whose son had waited on one of today's most famous Hollywood actors in a restaurant. As the boy continued to bring drinks, food, and refills to the table, he overheard the conversation the actor was having with his girlfriend. The bottom line was that this famous man was filling himself with a temporary tonic to ease his troubled soul. He was miserable, talking about how lonely and bored he was while trying to drown his problems in a shot glass.

There are millions like him—many even within the church. I identify with A. W. Pink, who said, "The change of emphasis in our writings has lost us hundreds of readers. Yet if we could relive the past fifteen years, we would follow the same course. The solemn days through which we are passing demand, as never before, that first things be put first. There are plenty of writers who cater to those who read for intellectual entertainment; our longing is to minister to those who yearn for a closer walk with God."[2]

My favorite story in the life of Elisha is found in 2 Kings 4:

> One of the wives of the sons of the prophets cried out to Elisha, "Your servant, my husband, has died. You know that your servant feared the LORD. Now the creditor is coming to take my two children as his slaves."
>
> Elisha asked her, "What can I do for you? Tell me, what do you have in the house?"
>
> She said, "Your servant has nothing in the house except a jar of oil."
>
> Then he said, "Go and borrow empty containers from everyone—from all your neighbors. Do not get just a few. Then go in and shut the door behind you and your sons, and pour oil into all these containers. Set the full ones to one side." So she left.
>
> After she had shut the door behind her and her sons, they kept bringing her containers, and she kept pouring. When they were full, she said to her son, "Bring me another container." But he replied, "There aren't any more." Then the oil stopped.
>
> She went and told the man of God, and he said, "Go sell the oil and pay your debt; you and your sons can live on the rest." (vv. 1–7)

How would you like for God to move in your life in such a way that there was—in place of desperation—an abounding sense of His power and presence? What would it do to you if God showed up and filled the empty corners of your heart? It would change your condition, your perspective, and probably your worship.

SPIRITUALLY SPEAKING

I grew up in a time when Southern Baptists were scared to talk about the Holy Spirit. I don't ever remember hearing a sermon on the Holy Spirit when I was growing up. I didn't hear much about the Holy Spirit at the Baptist college I attended, although I was a Bible major. I learned how to operate an overhead projector but rarely heard anyone talking about the victorious Christian life.

I really didn't understand the ministry of the Holy Spirit until I got to seminary and heard about it at a Bible conference I attended at the Red Bridge Baptist Church in Kansas City, Missouri. At that conference I was privileged to hear great and godly speakers of that day like Manley Beasley, Ron Dunn, Jack Taylor, and Bertha Smith. Miss Bertha was one of the most famous Southern Baptist missionaries and had written a book called *How the Spirit Filled My Life*. All were known at the time as "deeper life" teachers. But however you want to label them, they had a word from God to a young preacher whose well was empty.

A. W. Tozer wrote, "Evangelical Christianity believes it [the fullness of the Spirit] but nobody experiences it."[3] I long for more and more of the Spirit's power in my life. Too often I find that I talk about the Spirit more than I actually walk in the Spirit. Yet the New Testament teaches that it's my responsibility to walk in the Spirit. I am to be "filled with the Spirit" (Eph. 5:18). That's a command, not an option. If my vessel is empty, the problem is not God, it's me.

Think about what might be hindering the filling of your vessel today. Perhaps it stems from having too much confidence in your own ability to function without help, coupled with a lack of appreciation for what the Spirit can and will do for you. The Holy Spirit is not an additive; He's a necessity.

> **TOO OFTEN I FIND THAT I TALK ABOUT THE SPIRIT MORE THAN I ACTUALLY WALK IN THE SPIRIT.**

Another reason we fail to have full vessels is because we are resistant to repentance. We may know that we possess attitudes, actions, sins, habits, or desires that are inconsistent with the will and Word of God, but we justify them. Our tank is empty because we've not filled it up through repentance. Repentance brings restoration. Paul, writing to the church in Corinth, said, "Therefore dear friends, since we have such promises, we should wash ourselves clean from every impurity of the flesh and spirit, making our sanctification complete in the fear of God" (2 Cor. 7:1).

Others are empty because they cannot (or will not) take God at His word. They will not accept the desire of God to fill us with His Spirit by faith. If the widow in Elijah's day had tried to reason and rationalize the commands of the prophet, she and her two sons would have died. As we say in the South, there comes a time when you have to "fess up." You have to admit the problem and decide it's worth doing whatever it takes to make it right.

The Scriptures teach us that "faith comes by hearing, and hearing by the word of God" (Rom. 10:17 NKJV). That's the problem with what many people call "faith" in our culture. It's built on something other than a biblical definition. Truth and trust go hand-in-hand. The prophet spoke, but the widow had to act. As James so profoundly and succinctly stated, "Faith without works is dead" (James 2:26). This woman had to act on the word of God from the prophet of God. The sure word of Elisha had to be acted on to be effective. If you trust, then you naturally obey. George Duncan writes, "Faith is not based upon ignorance but upon knowledge, and that is true, but it is also true that faith will find itself called to venture beyond that which it knows."[4]

The widow of 2 Kings 4 was called to act in faith amid a very desperate situation. This godly woman had been married to a prophet who feared the Lord, but he had left her in serious debt. She was now destitute and in danger of losing everything. One of the issues causing people to be desperate today is the economy. Will I have enough to retire? What if I get sick and lose all my life savings in medical bills or nursing home care? This widow faced a similar situation, but she lived in an age without Medicare, Social Security, or welfare. She had nowhere to turn but to the prophet of God.

WHEN THE NIGHT JUST WON'T END

In the mid-1990s I met a fellow pastor, Jerry Pereira, who was serving at First Baptist Church in Swannanoa, North Carolina. Jerry's wife, Sally, is the daughter of T. W. Wilson, who served most of his ministry as a close friend, confidant, and co-worker of Billy Graham. Because of my relationship with Jerry and Sally, I got to meet T. W. and his wife, Mary Helen. After T. W. had a stroke, I went to his house one afternoon to pray with him. When he passed away, T. W. was honored by Christian leaders from all across the nation. Dr. Graham, among others, shared a testimony of his faithfulness to God.

Two years later as the family still grieved the loss of T. W., Jerry was diagnosed with a very rare, aggressive cancer. At the time Jerry was in his second term as president of the North Carolina Baptist State Convention. He was a leader in his denomination and often spoke around the country at the Billy Graham Schools of Evangelism.

Jerry turned fifty while taking chemotherapy treatments. Although he had battled and prayed for six months, he succumbed to the cancer in November 2003. His funeral was a celebration of his life and ministry.

A couple of days before Jerry died, Bev Shea and his wife visited him in the hospital. Bev got right down over Jerry's face and sang "Jesus Loves Me." Bev said, "This is for you, Jerry." It appeared that Jerry might not have the strength, but he looked into Bev's eyes and mouthed the words right along with him, affirming his belief—even in his agony—that Jesus did indeed love him.

Jerry left behind his wife and two daughters, Emily and Mary, whom he loved dearly. Life has not been easy for Sally. We often forget that when a woman has been a pastor's wife most of her life and her husband suddenly dies, there is not only the grief of death but also a total change in identity. Imagine the struggles and adjustments laid on a person in this situation. The church doesn't know what to do. The grieving spouse doesn't know what to do. It can lead to great stress and anxiety.

Besides losing her husband, Sally also lost her pastor, going through those dark days with neither to support her. Eventually she had to go to church, the place where most people find comfort during times of grief. But her heart broke a little more each time she saw someone else standing in the pulpit where her husband had stood for more than eighteen years. Sally knew the congregation was grieving also. She felt a sense of responsibility to them, but she had to hear discussions of interims and search committees. Sally desperately needed her friends, and her girls needed the stability of a loving church family.

Actually Sally was struggling with even more than just the loss of her husband. Before Jerry's death, the Pereiras had begun dealing with issues at home with one of their daughters. I remember a call they made to us a few years prior, asking us to pray for Mary. They saw signs that she was heading into rebellion. We interceded for her that she would return to Christ. I remember us talking about the acrostic PUSH: "Pray until something happens." After her father died, Mary's life spiraled rapidly downhill, further compounding Sally's grief. While Emily wanted to be a missionary, Mary *needed* one.

Sadly the years haven't gotten any easier for Sally. She has struggled as a single mom. She has gone through a dark, lonely valley, yet she has maintained her faith in Christ. In late 2007, I sent her an e-mail just to check on her. In January 2008 she responded with a message that reminded me of my need to pray even harder for her. Read carefully her honest, gut-wrenching e-mail reply to me. Maybe you will find yourself in a similar situation. This is the cry of a desperate woman, but also of a woman who looks to God for her supply and sufficiency.

> Life has been hellacious. Mary's husband tried to kill her right after Thanksgiving. I got a call at 2:00 a.m. from a hospital chaplain. It was like a nightmare. Her husband's been in jail ever since, but is due to get out February 1. He told her he'll kill her when he gets out. The chief judge told her to take self-defense and get a gun. How's that for our system? She and her two babies have been in hiding, then at Helpmate, then at Mother's, and now in a government subsidized apartment.
>
> We've all been sick through Christmas and since. The backdoor neighbor's huge tree fell on my house December 30 while Emily, her fiancé David, and I were at church singing the "Hallelujah Chorus." If we had been here, we could have been killed. It took out my new room and fence. Jerry and I tried for years to

get them to cut it, but they liked trees! I do too, but not in my house. It rained in and then snowed, and a big clump of mistletoe fell on my sofa. It shattered my Bethlehem nativity, but my little sign remained standing that says, "Be still and know that I am God." I do know that, or I would go under. I've been without a floor, a ceiling, a roof, and heat in that room since then. I am finally seeing progress, and they have finally boarded up the roof.

On Tuesday night of last week, I passed out while driving in Asheville. It's a miracle that I didn't kill anybody. They thought I was having a stroke or a heart attack. It was finally determined that it was a panic attack, migraine related. The doctor said I need to rid my life of stress, sleep more, and walk two miles a day. The following Saturday my brother's grandbaby had a two hour seizure and was in the ICU on a ventilator in Florida. That same night Mary was taken to the ER with a blood clot.

I was trying to get out the door on Sunday morning and drive for the first time since Tuesday to get the babies when my cell phone rang. It was Emily's fiancé calling to say that she was in the ER in Virginia. I thought I'd just drop dead. Four of our family members were in the hospital within a six-day period. We're all back home and better, but not 100 percent. It's been very tedious. You asked how we are. Now I've probably told you more than you wanted to know!

Someone reminded her recently that joy comes in the morning. She responded by saying, "I know that. I just didn't know how long the night would be."

My friend will come through because she knows Who to turn to, even when it seems the house is empty. She has the grounding and the faith to see this through. She is not sitting quietly in a rocking chair waiting for Jesus to come back. She is putting her hands to the plow and moving forward, even as she continues to grieve the home-going of her husband and the situation with her youngest daughter. She is trusting the Lord and listening for His Word.

> **ONLY WHEN WE BEGIN TO SEE GOD AS OUR SOURCE WILL WE FIND HIM TO BE THE SUPPLY.**

By the way, God's Word is a great place to turn when you hit bottom. Only when we begin to see God as our source will we find Him to be the supply. As long as we think we are the owners of our lives, we'll never understand what it means to be a steward. We'll find ourselves hoarding and living in fear because we wonder if we can hold on until the end. The widow was desperate enough that she came to the right source. If she hadn't, she would have died in destitution with her sons in slavery.

Don't we see that all around us today? Isn't that the trouble with many who are believers in Christ? They are living beneath their privilege. They possess all the riches in Christ, but they live like spiritual paupers. They think their best days are behind them. They can't imagine a positive future, so they wallow in fear, doubt, and self-pity. Their lives and countenances reflect defeat rather than hope. They aren't enjoying their salvation, yet a fountain flowing with living water and untapped resources is within their grasp!

John Wesley observed, "Sour godliness is the devil's religion. It does not owe its inception to truly spiritual people or to truly spiritual practice. I suspect that sour godliness originated among unhappy, semi-religious people who had just enough religion to make them miserable but not enough to do them good." I've met widows like that. I've met deacons, church members, pastors, and missionaries like that. They've got just enough of God to be miserable. They have yet to come to the point of desperation.

We have an active ministry to widows in our local church. Our deacons check on them on a regular basis and often are found doing odd jobs for them. The prophet Elisha was doing what our deacons do—taking care of a widow in need.

She cried out to Elisha. She was a godly woman, and her husband had been a godly man. A. W. Pink says her cry "indicates the pressure of her grief and the earnestness of her appeal to the prophet. . . . The Lord is pleased to bring some to the end of their own resources [so] that His delivering hand may be more plainly seen acting on their behalf."[5]

55

This widow's husband was most likely the breadwinner of the family. They had no life insurance or retirement plan. He was dead, and now everything was going to change. Disaster and sorrow had not ended after he was buried. There was the grief of seeing all she loved slip through her hands. Life had become a deathlike existence.

Reality can be brutal. At the same time, it can drive us into a new dimension of trust. It is important for us to remember that at some point we will all be desperate.

- Our job may be phased out by the corporation we've worked for all our lives.
- Our pension fund may dry up.
- The health we've enjoyed may fail us.
- The problems of the neighbors' kids may become the problems of our own kids.
- The doctor may come to us with that look of concern on his face.
- The phone may ring in the middle of the night heralding devastating news.
- The child you love may call to say she's getting a divorce.
- The church you've sweated, prayed, and worked for may tell you they want to go in a different direction.

Let's be honest. There is so much of life we can't control. We can't control the weather, the economy, terrorism, and a thousand other things. As long as we think we can control our lives, we can never experience the fullness of life as God intended. But when we resign as commander of the universe and throw ourselves in desperation before God, we then begin to see our vessels filled with resources previously unknown.

TOUGH TIMES, TOUGH CHOICES

I've lived long enough to see the housing market go up and down. Terri and I once owned a house and paid 13 percent interest—we were house poor. Twice in our marriage we've been stuck with two house payments because of moving to another church, and it took everything we had to keep from going under financially.

Much of the economic news recently has been about the housing and mortgage crises. Easy money and easy loans allowed many people who couldn't otherwise afford to buy a home to become homeowners. Almost daily, as the mortgage crisis has become the subject of presidential debates, congressional hearings, and economic programs, we hear of people losing it all. Some folks bought more than they could afford. Others made the tragic mistake of getting an interest-only loan and never paid anything but interest. When the market dropped, they owed more than their house was worth.

The 2 Kings widow was about to lose the roof over her head. She would be put out into the streets, and her sons would be sold into slavery. Their economic future was dim. According to Jewish law, the debt collector had a right to be at her door, but like most bill collectors, he lacked mercy or compassion. Here was a widow, looking down the barrel of a gun loaded with ruin, poverty, captivity, and bondage, with seemingly no way out.

Maybe you are desperate because you're in debt over your head. I would encourage you to seek financial counseling and establish a strict budget to get out of debt. More than that, however, I would encourage you to do perhaps the last thing you'd expect anyone to suggest: start tithing. Trust God with what you have. Believe God's plan of economy. After all, it was *your* financial planning that got you into this mess in the first place. Try God's for a change.

Maybe you are bankrupt spiritually. Your prayer life seems shallow, your walk is faltering, and your religious talk sounds hollow. You know more than you are living up to. It's time to get honest before the Lord. You need a divine intervention. You need a different solution than the one you've been looking for. You need God to show up at your door. This unnamed lady was about to lose her two children to slavery because of this debt. When you hit bottom, you'd better know where to turn.

Many have accepted trouble and feelings of emptiness as the norm. I heard Vance Havner say, "The church is so subnormal that if it ever got back to the New Testament normal, it would appear to be abnormal." We've gone too long accepting subnormal living as the normal Christian life, not only in our personal lives but also in the church.

It's time to get desperate!

The widow woke up to the reality of her condition. By turning to the prophet, she was turning to God for help. God is more than willing to come to our need and to be our supply. He is able to do "above and beyond all that we ask or think— according to the power that works in you" (Eph. 3:20).

Elisha asked her, "What do you have in the house?" He didn't offer financial counseling. He asked her simply to tell him what she had. Desperate people don't argue, debate, or dialogue. They do what they are told to do when God speaks. God was about to reverse her situation because she was willing to acknowledge her desperate need.

Most of us would have missed the miracle because we would have argued about the method God was using. After all, when you're at the point of no return, what's a little jar of oil going to do to rectify the situation?

Oil is often a symbol of the Holy Spirit in Scripture. The Spirit of God is looking for empty vessels to fill. He takes our little lives and then fills them to overflowing. Only He can change us from emptiness to fullness, from abasing to abounding. Look at how the widow responded to Elisha: "Your servant has nothing in the house except a jar of oil" (2 Kings 4:2). The word for "jar" here is a unique word. It means a small flask,

WALKING IN THE SPIRIT DEMANDS THAT YOU GO TO THE RIGHT SOURCE FOR YOUR SOLUTIONS.

just enough to hold the little amount of oil needed for anointing a body. It's a travel-sized vessel that would fit in an airplane carry-on bag. Not much, but just enough.

She went to the man of God seeking a word from God. She had a house full of problems, but she knew where to go when she was in trouble. Walking in the Spirit demands that you go to the right source for your solutions. It's not in trying, but in trusting.

I have the following notes written in my personal Bible as reminders of what a valuable commodity oil was in the Hebrew home during those times.

- It was used as fuel for light.
- It was frequently rubbed on wounds as a healing agent.
- In Leviticus 14:10, it was a major ingredient in the special offerings prescribed to announce the cleansing of a leper.
- It was used in cooking to add flavor.
- It was used to anoint kings as a symbol of God's authority.
- It was used to anoint priests and prophets.

Jill Briscoe writes,

> Another important symbol for the Holy Spirit's work in our lives is that of oil. Both now and in biblical times, oil is an important substance. It nourishes. It lubricates, makes things work better. It provides energy to our bodies and can be burned to provide light. It binds and soothes and unites. In the Bible, people or objects were anointed with oil for different reasons. Special oil was created for medicinal, preservative, and cosmetic objectives. It was also used for burning in lamps. God invested anointing oil with religious significance, too. . . . It speaks . . . of God's ability to help us live the life He calls

us to. And it tells us something about how He works in us.[6]

What's in your home that God can use? We so abuse the term "anointing" today, I'm fearful of using it. But the bottom line is, God wants to use us, fill us, and empower us. He is looking for vessels that have been to the bottom and have turned to Him for a fresh filling.

When God finds available vessels like you and me, He uses us to bring light to others who are going through dark times. He uses our words and actions to be healing agents to hurting people. He flavors a bland world by our lives. He allows us to stand in His authority and boldly proclaim the gospel of the King of kings.

Look at what happens when desperate people make themselves available. "Then he said, 'Go and borrow empty containers from everyone—from all your neighbors. Do not just get a few'" (2 Kings 4:3). God is looking for empty vessels He can fill. What you have is what God wants. The prophet was testing her faith and her willingness to obey. Too often we obey only if we can see how it's all going to work out. Elisha demanded she act on faith without seeing the reason behind his command. The essence of faith is obedience.

I love the story of this widow. She did what she was told. She listened to Elisha and believed his words of hope and deliverance. She didn't debate, discuss, or deliberate—she obeyed—completely. Apparently she went through the village or town and got every available jar she could find. She may have rummaged through the garbage, knocked on neighbors' doors, and even looked on the side of the road for a jar that had been dropped or cast aside. She got all she could because she was expecting something significant to happen.

The widow didn't call the local paper to come and watch. She didn't get on the local radio or television station to describe the jars. She did what she was told to do and shut the door. "Then go in and shut the door behind you and your sons, and pour oil into all these containers" (2 Kings 4:4). What Elisha commanded her to do probably sounded silly, but she did what he said.

SO WHAT ARE YOU GOING TO DO?

The key to getting hold of God is to get alone with Him. God seldom meets us in a crowd. He calls us out of the crowd and deals with us personally. Whether you are talking about Jacob wrestling with God, Moses at the burning bush, Elijah sitting under the tree, or even our Lord in Gethsemane, the key to power for the moment is getting alone with the Father. What the widow did, she did in the privacy of her home.

As you read this passage, you will note three times in this chapter a reference to the door being "shut." We can't be something in public that we aren't in private. My friend Roger Breland, founder of the contemporary Christian music group TRUTH, has always said, "If God is going to use you publicly, He has to tutor you privately." Jesus told us to come away and rest awhile. We are so busy running here and there, we have little time to shut the door and get alone with God. Therefore, our lives are not authentic and we lack power, all because we are not spending time with the Lord.

Notice that Elisha did not send the widow out to get full vessels but empty ones. It would have been man's solution to go to the neighbors and ask to borrow a couple of *full* jars of oil, but God's ways and man's ways are different. Think about it—she didn't have enough oil to fill even one vessel, much less all the jars she had gathered in her home. But she believed the prophet and did what he told her to do. Someone has said, "God can only fill you to the measure of your obedience. He will not do any more for you until you obey what He has already said for you to do."

Desperate people obey willingly. They've exhausted all other avenues and options. Verse 5 says it all in a very short space: "She poured." She didn't calculate; she just began to pour. She emptied herself of her pride only to find that the prophet's words were empowering her to have an abundance, beyond measure, overflowing, more than enough to meet all her needs. She did what was required and held nothing back. The result was a blessing she could have never obtained in any other way.

All other solutions would have been worldly, man-made, and would eventually run out. If she had done what mankind often does, she would have run out of oil again and been back in the same spot with the same problem. Never second-guess or underestimate the heart of God when it comes to meeting people at the point of their need. Let God fill you and use you to the fullest!

THAT'LL BE ENOUGH

Pick up the story once more in verse 6: "When they were full, she said to her son, 'Bring me another container.' But he replied, 'There aren't any more.' Then the oil stopped. She went and told the man of God, and he said, 'Go sell the oil and pay your debt; you and your sons can live on the rest'" (2 Kings 4:6–7). Her act of faith resulted in God answering her prayers and meeting her needs. Obedience delivered her from bondage, debt, and the bill collectors. Her sons would no longer be in danger of being sold into slavery. By her obedience she had obtained freedom for herself and her sons.

Why? Because she was willing to empty herself first. She shared her heart with Elisha, and he shared God's power and provision with her. John G. Butler says, "We see the wisdom in going to the Word for help in our problems, but how few see the need of going to the Word for instructions on what to do with their prosperity." By those few faith steps—gathering the vessels, shutting the door, pouring out the oil—the widow was able to move from defeat to victory. She was able to pay all her debts. And she stands today, thousands of years later, as a witness to the power and provision of God.

Paul said, "And my God will supply all your needs according to His riches in glory in Christ Jesus" (Phil. 4:19). *According* to His riches, not *out* of His riches. It's an endless supply. God will never run short of His own riches. There will never be a time when heaven can't meet you at the point of your need. When we walk in this truth, we are witnesses of the sufficiency of our sovereign Savior.

All the widow had to do was open the door and let folks see. A few hours earlier, she had been running here and there, trying to find vessels. Now she had a house that was full to meet all her needs and then some. When desperate people encounter the divine solution, they don't have to advertise. They just need to open the door, and people will come and see.

Take God at His word. Don't negotiate or try to figure it out. Have the attitude of the mother of Jesus who said to those at the wedding feast, "Do whatever He tells you" (John 2:5). End of discussion and the beginning of blessings.

CHAPTER 4

THE OBEDIENCE OF DESPERATION

2 Kings 5

The Bible recognizes no faith that does not lead to obedience, nor does it recognize any obedience that does not spring from faith. The two are opposite sides of the same coin.
—A. W. Tozer

This is how we know that we love God's children when we love God and obey His commands. For this is what love for God is: to keep His commands.
—1 John 5:2–3

BY NATURE we want God to fix our lives with the wave of a magic wand. We want a prayer a day to keep the devil away. When we say, "God is just a prayer away," we think that means "God relieving me of my pain is just a prayer away."

As I was getting ready to write this chapter, I was burning the candle at both ends. I had a book deadline to meet. As the presiding president of the Southern Baptist Convention's Pastors' Conference, I was in the final weeks of planning our annual meeting. On top of that, we were in the last stages of a $5 million dollar stewardship campaign at our church. Add to that the traveling to promote Sherwood Pictures' new movie *Fireproof*, as well as other outside speaking endeavors, and I was running in the fast lane. I didn't have time to stop, slow down, or even think.

During that time I began to feel the life drain out of me. I was exhausted; I just wanted to sit back, get a deep breath, and take a break. I was doing all I could to figure out how to get through the convention and maybe find a week to rest.

But God had other plans.

One night I started feeling pain in my stomach. I thought it was diverticulitis and tried to wrestle through the night with the pain, failing to get any sleep. The next morning I called my doctor, and she advised me to go to the emergency room. My wife and I arrived there around 10:00 a.m. By 1:30 that afternoon they were rolling me into surgery for an emergency appendectomy.

I was going to have time to rest, but not at the time of my choosing or the way of my choosing. As I sat at home recovering,

I was reminded that God doesn't need my gifts, my talents, or my titles. What He wants from me is my absolute obedience. I was placed in a position where I could not travel, did not feel like getting off the couch, and could not cover all the bases I felt needed to be covered. I had to learn to trust and obey. For a type A person, that's a tough thing to do.

I think Naaman was a type A person. He didn't have time to be sick. He was an important man in the army of Aram. He was considered a "great man in his master's sight and highly regarded . . . a brave warrior" (2 Kings 5:1). Some have said that he was the soldier at the battle of Ramoth Gilead whose shot killed Ahab, and thus Aram's victory was attributed to him.

But Naaman had a problem. He was all these things—and a leper. With his fame came fear. His power was accompanied by the discoloration of his skin and the open sores that ravaged his body. He was a hero in his land, but not one person in his country would have traded places with him.

Leprosy was a frightening disease in ancient times. According to the book of Numbers, lepers were required to live outside the city. They were considered unclean. At the time of Christ, lepers were to warn others of their approach by shouting, "Unclean!"

Although we hear little of leprosy these days, it is still a disease that affects our world. My father was stationed on the small island of Tinian during World War II. Tinian was the base where the *Enola Gay* took off with the first atomic bomb. It was one of the largest United States air bases in the Pacific, but after the war the island was turned into a leper colony.

My friend Roger Breland helped to establish two hospitals in Africa for children with leprosy in cooperation with the American Leprosy Mission. You can now completely cure one person of leprosy for only $300—a small price to pay to heal a disease once considered so ghastly. But we must remember that leprosy at the time of Naaman would have been considered like AIDS. People feared being contaminated or infected, thus they shied away from contact with anyone who carried the disease. What is curable today was deadly at that time.

God was going to cure the leper leader, but not the way Naaman anticipated. The great Physician's cure would leave no doubt that it was God actively at work in the situation. God would have to bring Naaman to a point of desperation, faith, and obedience for him to find the cure he sought.

CAN I HELP YOU?

Note that God used a variety of people to bring Naaman to this point. Naaman could have been considered a self-made man. He was a hero, a warrior, and a leader. But to have victory over his leprosy, he needed other people. As you read the text, you find seven individuals or groups of individuals who are part of the process, reminding us that no one gets to God on their own. While we do come to Christ alone by grace alone through faith alone, we are, in reality, in need of others to show us the way.

I heard a sermon recently where the speaker said it takes seven people to bring someone to Christ. He said, "It's not whether you are number one or number four or number seven;

God needs each of us to be one of seven in others' lives to get them to Jesus."

After thinking about that, I was reading T. S. Rendall's book *Elisha: Prophet of the Abundant Life*. In his chapter on Naaman, Rendall gives the seven links in the chain that resulted in the healing of Naaman. These seven were linked together in a way that led Naaman to obedient, believing faith.

1) *The little Jewish maid.* "Aram had gone on raids and brought back from the land of Israel a young girl who served Naaman's wife. She said to her mistress, 'If only my master would go to the prophet who is in Samaria, he would cure him of his skin disease'" (2 Kings 5:2–3).

2) *An unnamed individual.* "So Naaman went and told his master what the girl from the land of Israel had said" (v. 4).

3) *The king of Syria.* "Therefore, the king of Aram said, 'Go and I will send a letter with you to the king of Israel'" (v. 5).

4) *The king of Israel.* "When the king of Israel read the letter, he tore his clothes and asked, 'Am I God, killing and giving life that this man expects me to cure a man of his skin disease? Think it over and you will see that he is only picking a fight with me'" (v. 7).

5) *Elisha.* "When Elisha the man of God heard that the king of Israel tore his clothes, he sent a message to the king, 'Why have you torn your clothes? Have him come to me, and he will know there is a prophet in Israel'" (v. 8).

6) *Elisha's messenger.* "Then Elisha sent him a messenger, who said, 'Go wash seven times in the Jordan and your flesh will be restored and you will be clean'" (v. 10).

7) *Naaman's servant.* "But his servants approached and said to him, 'My father, if the prophet had told you to do some great thing, would you not have done it? How much more should you do it when he tells you, "Wash and be clean"?'" (v. 13).[1]

God's solution to Naaman's problem was revealed through others. Never underestimate the important role you might play in the life of another person. It may be you have a friend, family member, neighbor, or work associate like Naaman. Someone needs to point them in the right direction. Often God is their last resort, not their first option. When people are desperate and dying, it is no time for believers to be fearful of what others might think. It is time for us to obey God and act, asking Him to use us in the lives of others. Our obedience in allowing God to use us could put them on the path of obedience.

> **GOD IS NOT INTERESTED IN OUR SILVER AND GOLD; HE IS ONLY INTERESTED IN OUR HEARTS.**

Think of the servant girl. She was a slave, but she used her condition to serve God and thus bring deliverance to another. David Roper describes it this way:

> She said to her mistress, "If only my master would see the prophet who is in Samaria! He would cure him of his leprosy." The rabbis call attention to the particular construction of the sentence and render it, "If only the *supplications* (prayers) of my Master could be set before the prophet who is in Samaria." Naaman was

a hard man, but underneath was quiet desperation. He was dying, and there was nothing
anyone could do."[2]

One thing led to another, and finally Naaman found himself
at the door of the prophet's house. Naaman would have known
of the weird ways of the false prophets of his nation. He would
have known of the many gods who promised cures by chant-
ing, magic, and a variety of other methods. He was about to
encounter his first true prophet—a man of God with the power
to actually do something about Naaman's desperate situation.
The question would now be: Would Naaman listen? Would he
obey? Or would he deem the commands of the prophet beneath
someone of his status?

Naaman carried thousands upon thousands of dollars worth
of gold and silver, plus he brought the finest clothes imaginable.
Naaman showed up at the prophet's door thinking he could buy
the favor of God. Isn't that the way we think today? Ulterior
motives lead us to give in order to get! We give God our grocery
lists, expecting Him to do what we demand. But God is not
interested in our silver and gold; He is only interested in our
hearts.

The very fact that Naaman was willing to take the painful
and difficult journey to Israel shows that he was desperate. He
was admitting that the gods of his land had been unable to do
what the God of Israel could do. It was an admission of need,
yet with conditions. Being a proud man with a great reputation,
he easily obtained the king of Syria's permission to travel to

Israel. There he was given an audience with the king. He had brought some of the treasures of Syria with him, just in case he needed to pay for his healing. Paying for something means you don't owe anyone. You bought it, earned it, and deserved it. Having nothing to offer for what you need puts you in the position of humility. God was positioning Naaman to move from dignity to desperation. This healing would not come through silver and gold.

HEALING WITHOUT HUMILITY?

> So Naaman came with his horses and chariots and stood at the door of Elisha's house. Then Elisha sent him a messenger, who said, "Go wash seven times in the Jordan and your flesh will be restored and you will be clean." But Naaman got angry and left, saying, "I was telling myself: He will surely come out, stand and call on the name of Yahweh his God, and will wave his hand over the spot and cure the skin disease." (2 Kings 5:9–11)

Naaman expected special treatment. He expected to be courted, bowed down to, and respected. Couldn't Elisha just look out the window and see all those treasures? What else would a poor preacher want than a good retirement fund? He could call it quits at any time with no worries or fears if he just met Naaman on Naaman's terms. After all, he was a leader and a warrior at the home of a mangy old prophet. Surely the prophet was desperate for cash.

Naaman arrived with all the pomp and circumstance of a high official. He probably expected Elisha to roll out the red carpet and bring out the fine china. As a hero in his land, he had a letter from the king of Syria (which apparently Elisha never bothered to read).

Naaman couldn't conceive of a scenario where his arrival— leprosy and all—would not command awe and respect. But Elisha was totally unimpressed with the chariots of Naaman. This prophet was not a healer for hire.

What could a man who had nothing possibly offer to a man who had everything? Yet Elisha was the doorway because he held what Naaman so desperately needed: healing. A cure from a deadly disease. Deliverance from the shame of a decaying body.

The fact that Elisha did not go out to greet him must have also added insult to injury. The prophet sent his *assistant* to talk to the renowned captain. That's right, a mere messenger gave orders to this great military leader: "Go wash seven times in the Jordan." Naaman was furious and stormed off. After traveling day and night to the home of Elisha, he left in haste because he hadn't received the answer he wanted. Naaman didn't want to obey. He just wanted healing on his terms, in his way, at his time.

Naaman's attitude is so different from that of the centurion during the time of Christ. Matthew 8 tells the story:

When He entered Capernaum, a centurion came to Him, pleading with Him, "Lord, my servant is lying at home paralyzed, in terrible agony!"

"I will come and heal him," He told him.

"Lord," the centurion replied, "I am not worthy to have You come under my roof. But only say the word, and my servant will be cured. For I too am a man under authority, having soldiers under my command. I say to this one, 'Go!' and he goes; and to another, 'Come!' and he comes; and to my slave, 'Do this!' and he does it."

Hearing this Jesus was amazed and said to those following Him, "I assure you: I have not found anyone in Israel with so great a faith!" (vv. 5–10)

A centurion was a Roman officer, most likely a tested and decorated soldier and leader, who commanded more than one hundred men. The rank and file would have respected him greatly. This centurion was called to serve in the barren land of Israel, far from Rome. It was an outpost no one would have wanted. If this man had not been there, however, he couldn't have met Christ. Circumstances and forces beyond himself brought him to the land and ultimately to the Lord.

Compare the response of Naaman with that of the centurion. Naaman came expecting to be honored; the centurion came bringing honor. In both situations we find a powerful Gentile confronting a lowly Jew. The difference in these encounters is that the centurion had faith, but Naaman had not yet been broken to the point of desperate seeking.

"But only say the word," is a far cry from riding off in a huff because you didn't get your way. The centurion knew there was something about Jesus that was different from anyone he had ever encountered. Both men were men of authority who exercised power over others. The centurion knew that his authority was an ability to direct men and demand their obedience. He also knew that Jesus had the authority to direct the forces of heaven to heal his

WE STAND OUTSIDE THE DOOR OF DELIVERANCE AND DEMAND THAT GOD COME OUT AND MEET US ON OUR TERMS.

paralyzed servant. Perhaps he had observed other miracles and believed by faith. One man was quick to obey while the other was reluctant.

I often find that the one factor hindering people from following God is obedience. They want to negotiate with the Lord. They expect preferential treatment because they are active members of a local church, they give lots of money, or they are influential in the community. Rarely do you find the "simply to the cross I cling" mentality in the body of Christ. We struggle with trust and resist the call to obey. We stand outside the door of deliverance and demand that God come out and meet us on our terms. We expect Him to recognize us even when we fail to recognize Him as sovereign and sufficient.

Ron Dunn wrote an excellent devotional entitled "Trust and Obey," in which he said:

> A car may have a tank full of gasoline, but unless the fuel is ignited it won't move an inch. I know many Christians whose tanks are full but they are still stalled between the Red Sea and the Jordan River. For years I was puzzled by members of my church who knew the Bible like scholars, could hear a sin drop a mile away, traveled hundreds of miles to attend Bible conferences, but whose lives lacked the pulse of Christ-likeness. In spite of all their knowledge and activity there was no sign of spiritual maturity; love, joy, peace, and other characteristics of a spiritual life were conspicuously absent. They had plenty of fuel—hi-test stuff—but no spark to ignite it.
>
> The purpose and timing of God constitute the fuel of victory in the Christian life. And the spark that ignites it, releasing it as a practical and powerful force in the life, is *obedience*. God's power flows in the stream of our obedience.
>
> Obedience is our responsibility. Even though the ability to obey comes from God, we, and we alone, are accountable for obedience. When the time is right, God reveals to us

His purpose, then says, "Now it's your move." And at that moment, everything hinges upon our obedience.

Obedience is the evidence and expression of our faith in God. Obedience is faith turned inside out. Faith is the seed, and obedience is the flower that springs from it. Faith is the root; obedience is the fruit. There is a very interesting passage of Scripture in Hebrews 3. The inspired author is recounting Israel's failure to enter Canaan.

"And to whom did He swear they would not enter His rest, but to those who were disobedient? So we see that they were not able to enter because of unbelief." (Heb. 3:18–19 NASB).

In verse 18, he says they couldn't enter because of disobedience; in verse 19, he says unbelief was the cause. Well, which was it—disobedience or unbelief? It was both. For obedience and faith are two sides of the same coin. You act on what you believe and you obey whom you trust. If you were to ask the Sunday morning worshipers if they believe the Bible from cover to cover, probably all would say they do. Yet the truth is, you believe only as much of the Bible as you are obeying! What you don't obey, you don't believe.

If we are reluctant to give unquestioning obedience to God, it is because we don't really trust Him. If obedience comes from trust, where does trust come from? And the answer is—knowledge. You won't obey someone you don't trust. You can't trust someone you don't know. So here is the spiritual equation for obedience: *knowledge of God equals faith in God equals obedience to God.*[3]

WHEN EXCUSES WON'T HOLD WATER

Naaman was not initially inclined to do what he was supposed to do. "'Aren't Abanah and Pharpar, the rivers of Damascus, better than all the waters of Israel? Could I not wash in them and be clean?'" (2 Kings 5:12). That's the voice of pride and selfishness from one who has not yet reached desperation.

Charles Spurgeon, one of the greatest preachers of all time, delivered a message on February 5, 1869, at Exeter Hall entitled, "Mr. Evil Questioning Tried and Executed." His text was 2 Kings 5:12. Though the language may seem dated, the truth is as relevant as tomorrow's headlines.

> Proud Self and Evil Questioning are two of Satan's firmest allies, and two of the chief destroyers of the souls of men. Both of these adversaries attacked Naaman at once. Proud Self fell upon him and gave him the first blow, and Naaman cried, "Behold, I thought, he will

surely come out to me, and stand and call on the name of the Lord his God, and strike his hand over the place and recover the leper." When Proud Self had given his blow, on came his friend and helper, Evil Questioning, and he smote Naaman, and then Naaman said, "Are not Abanah and Pharpar, rivers of Damascus, better than all the waters of Israel? May I not wash in them and be clean?" Ah! It is a hard case with a man who has to fight with two such imps as these—his own proud spirit, and that equally wicked spirit of unbelief—asking questions—evil questions—and tempting the Lord our God. Against the first, namely, our proud and righteous self, God has opened all his batteries. The ten commands are like ten great pieces of ordnance, every one of them pointed against our own pride and self-righteousness. The Bible is an opponent, even unto death, of everything like boasting, or encouraging the hope of salvation by any efforts of our own. Righteous Self is doomed to be rent in pieces, and his house to be made a dunghill; God hates him because he is an anti-Christ, and sets himself in opposition to the plenteous atonement of the Lord Jesus Christ. As for Evil Questioning, he also doth much ruin among the souls of men.

Listen to what Evil Questioning said to Naaman, and what Naaman said as the result of it. If I understand my text aright, it means just this: "What virtue can there be in water? Why should I be told to go and wash at all? I have washed many times and it never cured my leprosy. This dry disease is not so readily got rid of; but supposing there is some medical influence in water, why must I wash in Jordan? It is but a mere ditch, why can I not go and wash in some of my own rivers? We have medicinal streams in our own land. At any rate, Abanah and Pharpar are cleaner and wider, and their current is stronger than that of the Jordan, which empties itself into the Dead Sea. And to my mind," he says, "it seems to be but a dead river at the very best. May I not go home to Samaria and there wash? A pretty thing that I should come all this way from Samaria to see and then all he should tell me should be, wash and be clean. It is absurd," he says, "it is contrary to the nature of things; it cannot be possible, and therefore," he says, "I will not go and try it." This, you see, was Evil Questioning. What business was it of

IF HE WERE TO EXPLAIN HOW EVERYTHING WORKS OUT, THEN FAITH AND OBEDIENCE WOULDN'T BE REQUIRED.

Naaman's whether there was any medicinal powers in the water or not? What concern was it to him whether Abanah or Pharpar were better or worse than Jordan? He need have nothing to do but with the simple command— "Go, wash in Jordan seven times, and thou shalt be clean." 'Twas his to obey, not to question. 'Twas his to fulfill the command, not to enquire into its philosophy.[4]

Common sense can kill faith. Reasoning and questioning the Word and will of God will destroy faith and justify disobedience. Left to ourselves, we will argue with God and debate with Him regarding His methods. There's a difference between common sense and coming to your senses. When you come to your senses in the spiritual sense, you begin to understand that God's ways are not your ways. God doesn't have to explain Himself. If He were to explain how everything works out, then faith and obedience wouldn't be required.

- God told Noah to build a boat and spend 120 years doing so, even though it had never rained.
- God told Moses to cross the Red Sea and walk across on dry land. But it's hard to believe God can part the waters until you stand back and see the salvation of God.
- God told the Israelites to follow the ark into the Jordan. Then, and only then, would it dry up and permit them to cross.

- God told Joshua and the people of Israel to merely walk around Jericho and sound the trumpets, and the walls would fall.
- God told David to conquer the formidable Goliath with a few smooth stones and a slingshot.
- God told Mary she would give birth to the Son of God, even though she had never been with a man.
- And God continues to do impossible things through ordinary people!

JUST DO IT

We need people in our lives who will tell us the truth. We don't need gurus; we need godly people who are unafraid to come alongside and tell us what we need to do. Read again 2 Kings 5:13–14: "But his servants approached and said to him, 'My father, if the prophet had told you to do some great thing, would you not have done it? How much more should you do it when he tells you, "Wash and be clean"?' So Naaman went down and dipped himself in the Jordan seven times, according to the command of the man of God. Then his skin was restored and became like the skin of a small boy, and he was clean."

Naaman was like many believers today. They want God to work in their lives in miraculous ways, but they don't want to surrender to God's methods. Elisha's messenger didn't bargain, barter, or compromise. He said, "Go do this and you'll be clean." Someone once said that Naaman came to Elisha as a general who happened to be a leper; Elisha dealt with Naaman as a leper who happened to be a general.

The command was specific: Go wash in the Jordan—not in the place of your choosing. Dip yourself seven times—if you don't dip seven times, there is no cure. And the command demanded obedience and faith. Naaman had to go and do as he was told.

Warren Wiersbe notes, "Elisha didn't ask him to do something difficult or impossible, because that would only have increased his pride. He asked him to obey a simple command and perform a humbling act, and it was unreasonable not to submit. When Naaman told his story back in Syria and got to this point, his friend would say, 'You did what?' Faith that doesn't lead to obedience isn't faith at all."[5]

Like all of us, Naaman had to humble himself before the Lord. He had stormed off, but now he must get off his high horse and submit himself completely to the plan of God. When he obeyed God, he came out of the water healed.

There are several key lessons here regarding the obedience of desperation. First, when godly people speak into your life, listen. I'm not talking about people who have a hunch or a notion, but people who are in the Word and abiding in Christ. God has put them in your path to point you in the right direction. Heed their words.

Next, confirm their words with the Word of God. Don't buy into the "God told me to tell you" theology. I've often had people say something similar to me, although I knew they weren't walking with God. I realize God has spoken through a donkey, but only once. God *always* confirms His Word. He will give us the peace of God and the God of peace when we think biblically about our situation. Others have journeyed down this path. General principles about how to relate to God in your moment of desperation are revealed in God's Word.

Also, don't try to bargain with God. Naaman tried to hedge his bets and bring some money in case there was a cost involved by going to this faith healer. Elisha elicited nothing from him except complete obedience. God can't be bought. His truth can't be negotiated. God doesn't work according to the wisdom of men.

Finally, don't delay. Act when God says to act. "Go wash seven times in the Jordan." Elisha didn't ask Naaman to call an advisory board. He simply said, "Go!"

In his book *Slaying the Giants in Your Life*, David Jeremiah writes:

> A scholar once surveyed the Scripture to discover the most significant words in all the Bible. He wanted to find the saddest word, the happiest word, the most emotional word, and so on. When he came around to the Bible's most dangerous word, he identified it as "tomorrow." The word is a thief, he said, that robs dreamers of their dreams and the talented of their greatest achievements. It keeps men and women from coming to Christ and discovering the life God longs for them to have. The prince of preachers, Charles H. Spurgeon, agreed. "Tomorrow, Tomorrow, Tomorrow!" he

wrote. "Alas, tomorrow never comes! It is in no calendar except the almanac of fools."[6]

We are not promised another day or another breath. Respond to God in immediate and complete obedience and find healing and rest for your soul.

CHAPTER 5

ADMITTING OUR DESPERATE NEED FOR GOD

The Psalms

I will never despair, because I have a God;
I will never presume, because I am but a man.
—Owen Feltham

God, You are my God; I eagerly seek You.
I thirst for You; my body faints for You in a
land that is dry, desolate, and without water.
—Psalm 63:1

I'M A TYPE A PERSONALITY. Because of the strength of my flesh, I tend to want to help God out. If I am not careful, I will find myself looking to the Lord as a last resort instead of my first option. I'm an "I-can-fix-this" guy. Usually, however, I try and fail. That's because God isn't pushing me to *fix* it; He's pushing me to *faith* it. Even as I write, I can think of a dozen pastoral or personal illustrations of times when I've tried to help God out.

Our flesh has a hard time admitting need. We see it played out in everyday life. Couples refuse to get counsel and end up divorced because they say they can "fix it" without intervention. Relationships between friends become frayed because they think they can "fix it" by ignoring the issues. The hardest thing for any of us to admit is that we need help. Admitting we can't is the first step toward admitting He can.

Paul's words to the Romans are applicable on a number of levels. "There is no one righteous, not even one; there is no one who understands, there is no one who seeks God" (3:10–11). While we often try to apply these verses to unbelievers, they are tragically true of believers as well. Paul is unequivocal in his statement—not one, no one, not even one. It's an open and shut case.

Until we admit our need for God—that there is no good thing in us—we'll always try to figure it out on our own. We must come to the point where we recognize that we can't get ourselves out of the holes we've dug. Like the prodigal son, we may know in our heads that the Father wants what's best for us, but too often we choose the pigpen of self-sufficiency and self-will.

David often found himself crying out to God for help. David was a strong leader and a decisive man, but throughout the Psalms we often see him wrestling: Why has God abandoned me on the back side of the desert? Why do my enemies seem to be getting away with their actions against the Lord?

In Psalm 60:1, David said, "God, You have rejected us; You have broken out against us." His words are piercingly honest. God can always work with an honest person. In the first four verses of Psalm 60, we find the phrase "You have" repeated eight times. David clearly understood that Israel's initial defeat was the result of their unfaithfulness, and that God had gotten their attention through chastisement, discipline, and defeat.

In the following chapter, David talked about his heart being faint. Probably written at the time of his son Absalom's rebellion, he cried out to God to hear his prayer. David's heart was heavy. His son had rebelled against him. Life had thrown him a pitch impossible to hit.

Today as I was preparing to write this chapter, I was having a discussion with two of our staff members about godly people who have ungodly children. The conversation shifted to godly young people and couples who have no spiritual heritage. It doesn't make sense. Neither of these scenarios has a sensible explanation. Honestly, there is no magic formula. David was not a perfect parent. He had a rebellious and self-centered son who broke his heart. But before we start pointing out David's faults, let's remember that God, the perfect Father, gave a perfect environment to our parents, Adam and Eve, and they still chose sin over sanctuary in God's garden.

When David asked God to "give heed" to his cry (Ps. 61:1 NASB), the phrase carries the idea of hearing, and also the desire for action. David wanted God not only to hear his prayers but also to act on his prayers. David was desperate, and in his despair he cried out to the Lord.

In saying his heart was faint and "without strength" (Ps. 61:2), David was acknowledging that he was overwhelmed. He felt swamped by his circumstances. Although he knew he was God's man, this knowledge didn't change the hurt in his heart. David longed to get above the battle to the rock of security. He couldn't get there on his own; he needed God to lead him there.

In Psalm 62, David was facing a time of trouble so deep and burdensome that he had nothing to say. He simply waited in silence for God. No other counsel would suffice. No remedy could cure his hurting soul except that God should intervene as redeemer and refuge. As David writes, it is obvious that he wants to remind himself, as well as those who would later sing this psalm, that our faith should only be in the Lord.

Too often we put our faith in methods, programs, people, advice columns, horoscopes, Oprah, Dr. Phil, or even our favorite preacher. It is God and God alone that we must turn to. The advice of friends can encourage us in the moment, but often it cannot sustain us for the long haul. God must be our chosen object of faith. We must rely on Him, even when we want to find a few folks who will tell us what we want to hear, not what we *need* to hear.

David reminds us in Psalm 62:8, "Trust in Him at all times,

you people; pour out your hearts before Him. God is our refuge." When God hides Himself or seems indifferent to our struggles, it's hard to trust Him. Being the impatient people we are, we want quick answers and simple solutions to difficult problems. We want small bandages to cover deep wounds.

Waiting time is never wasted time, however, even though it may seem so at the moment. When I'm forced to wait, I'm forced to surrender my ideas and thoughts to God's sovereignty. I'm a talker. It's hard for me to be quiet. A friend of mine told me about being on a panel discussion with some very godly and distinguished people. He wrote himself a note: "KQYD—Keep Quiet, You Dummy." He said, "I stared at that note the whole time I continued to talk." I've been there and done that. "Be still and know I am God" is one of the hardest verses for most of us to practice.

They say silence is golden and talk is cheap. Speculation isn't worth a penny. We can play "what if" games in our minds until we drive ourselves crazy, but these games solve nothing. God was silent as Job sought answers. Finally when God spoke, it wasn't exactly what Job wanted to hear, but it was what he needed to hear.

THE SONG OF DESPAIR

In Psalm 63 we find a man of God who is seeking God at a deeper level than most of us have ever imagined. Again, this psalm was also probably written at the time of Absalom's rebellion. David had been driven into the wilderness. He prayed, "God, You are my God; I eagerly seek You. I thirst for You; my body faints for You in a land that is dry, desolate, and without water" (v. 1).

One of my favorite books to recommend to pastors is Jim Cymbala's *Fresh Wind, Fresh Fire*. It is one of the most encouraging books I've ever read. Jim shares the story of a wilderness time he and his wife Carol experienced when their daughter Chrissy started to rebel during her teenage years. He relates the agony of the nights when they didn't even know where she was. No matter how hard they prayed, their daughter seemed more distant. Jim admits that he was hanging on by a thread.[1]

> **DAVID DIDN'T MIND-LESSLY WRITE SONGS OF PRAISE THAT IGNORED THE ISSUES. HE WAS GOD-HONEST.**

At the same time, Carol was facing surgery. The enemy was bombarding them on every side. The accuser of the brethren seemed to be working overtime on them personally. At one of their lowest points, Carol wrote one of my favorite songs from the Brooklyn Tabernacle Choir, speaking of fears and tears, of weakness and worry, and yet declaring through the thick mist of despair that God had proved faithful. When it all seems lost, God can still be found.

David could have easily penned similar words. Although we often find David in a quandary, he rarely wrote a psalm that didn't end up proclaiming God's faithfulness, regardless of the circumstances. In our problems we must learn to praise. In our desperation we must find ways to delight in the Lord. Our focus can mean the difference between living in fear or in faith.

The wilderness of Judea is a barren land; very little can be found to sustain life. It is a treacherous, dangerous place where only the strong survive. Surely being out in the open in this howling expanse made David's spirit feel even more exhausted and his heart heavy, broken, and grieving as he longed for Jerusalem. As he penned these words, he could remember the good times in the sanctuary. He could recall those moments when he was riding high spiritually, when God's power and glory were so thick, a person could cut the air with a knife. Now he was in the wilderness—hot, dry, and a long way from the cool breezes of Jerusalem.

The thing I appreciate about David is that he didn't write pie-in-the-sky songs. He knew life on the mountaintop as well as in the valley. His honesty has brought comfort to millions of struggling saints for centuries.

Some of his psalms were written during times when it seemed the wind was always at his back, the favor of God upon every decision he made. Others were written, however, when it seemed that every wind brought a storm roaring into his life. Times when he was weary, hungry, or lacking any appetite, when life had a bitter taste. David didn't mindlessly write songs of praise that ignored the issues. He was God-honest. That's one reason we love him. That's one reason these songs with tunes long since forgotten can still bring a hopeful song to our hearts. Their melodies of truth ring in a major key in our hearts, even when we are living in a minor key moment.

Although David was in the desert, he had not lost his ability to hit the high notes. This great singer and songwriter still knew how to soar to the heavenlies to renew his heart. The landscape may have been flat, but his heart would always tune itself to the heart of God. When he couldn't sleep, he could still lie in bed singing of the goodness of God.

"My lips will glorify You because Your faithful love is better than life" (Ps. 63:3). Stop and think about that phrase and apply it right now to your life. *Your faithful love is better than . . . (fill in the blank).* Paul said, "For me, living is Christ and dying is gain" (Phil. 1:21). What about you? *For me, to live is* _____ *and to die is* _____.

Let's admit it here and now: one of the reasons God takes us through dark times is because, for us, "to live" is something or someone else other than Christ. "To die" is loss for us, not gain.

Can you see the progression of David's soul throughout Psalm 63? He senses "thirst," yet admits that God can "satisfy," so "I follow close to you." Lamoyne Sharpe writes, "It is important to notice that David's soul does not thirst for water, nor for the blood of his enemies, nor for deliverance out of this dry and barren land, nor for a crown and a kingdom; but his soul thirsted for God. David longed for the power and glory of God to be manifested. He had set his affections on things above and not on the things of earth. Our problem is that we thirst too little for spiritual things and too much for material and physical things."[2]

David had a craving, a thirst in his heart for God. What he had learned in worship was now being tested and proven in the wilderness. It is good to remember the times of blessings when we are in the times of barrenness. We tend to forget; that's why Moses told the people to remember. We must remember that God uses the wilderness to get our undivided attention. And to write songs in our heart whose lyrics can only be discovered in despair.

WILDERNESS PASSION

David declared in Psalm 63:1, "You are my God." Note the personal pronouns. You are mine. You and You only. I am looking to no other. I don't have a backup plan. Being pursued by a rebellious son did not stop him from pursuing God. He would seek the Lord, not halfheartedly but earnestly. His pursuit of God was like that of a man with an unquenchable thirst. *The Message* translates the verse this way: "I can't get enough of you! I've worked up such hunger and thirst." David was exiled from the throne but not from God.

In four decades of ministry, I've found many believers who have never pursued God with that kind of desire. They seek God when it's convenient. The average member of my denomination only makes it to church half the time, if they make it at all. Yet they expect the pastor and staff to come running the first time they have a runny nose. That's the problem with Americanized Christianity—we think we can pursue God at our convenience. We have little hunger and thirst for God.

More times than I can tell, I have stood in a nursing home or by the bedside of a dying person to hear them recount the regrets of a wasted life. They came to a hard place in their life, and rather than turning to the Lord, they turned away from

Him. They became angry with God and blamed Him for their hardship. Unfortunately they never took an honest look at themselves in the mirror of God's Word, yet they expected a dead faith to work in a time of crisis.

I've also found that the most dishonest people on the planet are God's people. We fear sharing our hearts and our burdens with others lest they think we are not spiritual. We worry about the opinions of others, about maintaining our façades more than getting before God. That's why there are so few today who have a heart like David.

Again, I want to go back to the story of the Cymbala family and their daughter Chrissy. One night Jim approached the prayer meeting crowd and said, "My daughter is very far from God these days. She thinks up is down, and down is up; dark is light and light is dark. But I know God can break through to her, and so I'm going to ask Pastor Boekstaff to lead us in praying for Chrissy."

As Jim tells it, "Thirty-two hours later, as I was shaving, Carol suddenly burst through the door, her eyes wide. 'Go downstairs!' she blurted, 'Chrissy's here.' Chrissy *was* there. She started confessing her sin and asking for forgiveness. Then she said, 'Daddy, who was praying for me? On Tuesday night, Daddy, who was praying for me? In the middle of the night, God woke me up and showed me I was heading toward this abyss. . . . But at the same time, it was like God wrapped his arms around me and held me tight.'"[3]

When's the last time you went to your prayer closet and got honest with God? When's the last time you stopped with

ADMITTING OUR DESPERATE NEED FOR GOD

the doughnuts and coffee and begged your Sunday school class to intercede for your family? I'm not talking about bleeding all over the front of your church and sharing gory details. I'm talking about being honest before God and others about the fact that you are hurting.

I have several prayer warriors I call on when my heart is heavy. I know they understand how to get hold of God for me or for the situation I'm facing. They bombard heaven on my behalf. I have shared things with them that keep me from looking "good" in their eyes, but I'd rather them know I am frail flesh than to live in the flesh, in my own strength. I don't want to live my life depending on what I can figure out. I know that victory is found in a daily admission of my need for Him.

WILDERNESS WORSHIP

Psalm 100 is a song of hope in which David writes words of encouragement and praise.

> Shout triumphantly to the LORD, all the earth. Serve the LORD with gladness; come before Him with joyful songs. Acknowledge that the LORD is God. He made us, and we are His—His people, the sheep of His pasture.
>
> Enter His gates with thanksgiving and His courts with praise. Give thanks to Him and praise His name. For the LORD is good and His love is eternal; His faithfulness endures through all generations.

This is a psalm of praise from beginning to end. The two stanzas call us to praise God passionately and continually for who He is and what He does.

We are taught five times in these verses that praise, joy, and gladness are to be part of our lives through five expressions of worship:

- Exhortation—"Shout triumphantly" (v. 1)
- Exultation—"Serve the LORD with gladness; come before Him with joyful songs" (v. 2)
- Explanation—"Acknowledge that the LORD is God . . . we are His" (v. 3)
- Expression—"Enter His gates with thanksgiving. . . . Give thanks to Him and praise His name" (v. 4)
- Extension—"His love is eternal; His faithfulness endures through all generations" (v. 5)

David also communicates the following seven imperatives through this psalm:

- Shout triumphantly—not just screaming but joyful shouting to the Lord.
- Serve the Lord—not begrudgingly or halfheartedly but with gladness.
- Come before Him—not just with repetitious singing but joyful singing.
- Enter His gates—come into His church with a thankful heart.

- Enter His courts—come into His presence with a spirit of worship, not a spirit of grumbling.
- Give thanks to Him—let your heart overflow with gratitude to the Lord.
- Praise His name—with the whole body of believers, bless His name corporately.

When we truly acknowledge our desperate need for God, we will respond with adoration, just like David did in Psalm 100. Our holy God deserves to hear from happy people. We have been pardoned from our sins by the substitutionary death of Jesus Christ on our behalf. That's something we desperately need, and it's worthy of our loud praise!

When we realize the abundance of God's gracious gifts bestowed on our unworthy lives, we will approach Him with willing hearts. Our service will be motivated by glad hearts—not out of duty but out of overflowing delight. Jesus Himself modeled this attitude through His selfless service of others. We should do the same.

When we're desperate for God, we aren't desperate for the spotlight. A spirit of genuine humility will cover what we do because we've got nothing to lose and nothing to prove.

Leonard Bernstein was asked, "What is the most difficult instrument to play?" He replied, "Second fiddle. I can get plenty of first violinists, but to find one who plays second violin with as much enthusiasm or second French horn or second flute, now that's a problem. And yet if no one plays second, we have no harmony."

In this world of self-worship, our desperation for God drives us to our knees in worship before the only One worthy of our praise. We're surrounded by those who worship their bodies or their favorite team or celebrity icons. Unfortunately the things that we worship apart from Christ are fleeting. They pay us no attention, and our worship only serves to pad their pockets and boost their egos.

In 1 Corinthians 6 Paul reminds us of the importance of not glorying in our flesh: "Do you not know that your body is a sanctuary of the Holy Spirit who is in you, whom you have from God? You are not your own, for you were bought at a price; therefore glorify God in your body" (vv. 19–20). Desperation for Christ opens wide the door of access to the throne of grace.

> **BY OUR HEARTFELT WORSHIP OVERFLOWING FROM LIVES OF DESPERATION, WE AFFIRM THE GOODNESS OF THE LORD.**

When people visit the White House or the Executive Offices for meetings, they have to go through an extensive background check. When they finally arrive, they must stop at the gate and talk to a uniformed Secret Service agent and then go through a metal detector scan. To gain access, one has to go through a lot of legal red tape.

Access to God, however, has already been granted to us through the blood of Christ. We are pre-approved. The writer of Hebrews exhorts us to "approach the throne of grace with boldness, so that we may receive mercy and find grace to help us at the proper time" (4:16). God's Word is full of promises for those who will draw near to Christ (see John 6:37, 51; 7:37; 10:9–10; 15:5).

An all-access pass like the one we've received in Christ should be accompanied by grateful hearts. Thanksgiving ought to be the theme of our worship before the throne. When David penned the words to Psalm 100, he had the Old Testament temple in mind. The temple courts allowed thousands to gather for worship. David encouraged his readers to enter the temple with loud shouts and songs, openly praising God. When we do this today, those on the outside looking in will see the difference Christ has made in our lives.

Our lives should be living, breathing expressions of praise— at home, at work, at school, in our neighborhood, with our friends and family. I'm not talking about bumper sticker, T-shirt faith. I'm talking about real faith working itself out in real life.

By our heartfelt worship overflowing from lives of desperation, we affirm the goodness of the Lord. God's goodness is one of our strongest motivations for living right and staying right. When we get a clear glimpse of how gracious and patient our good God has been with us, we will long to live holy lives that honor Him.

I used to hear Vance Havner say, "It's one thing to say Jesus is all you want, until He's all you've got, and then you discover He's all you ever needed." Only the desperate cry out to God. The self-satisfied *cannot,* and the self-sufficient *will* not. Notice the characteristics of those whom Jesus blesses in the beatitudes from Matthew 5—the poor in spirit, those who mourn, the gentle, the pure in heart, those who hunger and thirst for righteousness, the persecuted. These descriptions are a far cry from the exalted "self-made man" of our postmodern generation.

I remember a visit we made to the Church of the Nativity in Bethlehem. After walking across an open market, you go through a very small entrance that forces you to duck down to get into the church. Centuries ago the local rulers would ride into town on their horses with pomp and grandeur. The priests thoughtfully lowered the height of the door, so people would have to stoop to enter.

To enter the presence of God, we must stoop. We've got to die to self and get desperate.

As I said, I've spent too many years trying to help God out. At times in the past, I have needed a fresh touch or word from God, but I was too busy striving in my flesh. A few years ago during a conference in Tampa, I was alone in my hotel room. I sat at the desk and stared into the mirror, and I heard God say, "I don't like you very much. You've become a median adult." I, too, had to admit that my heart's desire at the time was to coast. I was tired and stressed and had settled for second best in my life. That day was a defining moment for me, a rekindling of the flame on a journey of desperation. I had come to the end of myself. No longer was I going to continue offering God my lousy favors by "helping" Him out.

Years ago at the Moody Bible Conference, Alistair Begg was preaching about King Jehoshaphat from 2 Chronicles 20. The king faced an overpowering enemy, and he called the people to prayer and fasting. Jehoshaphat prayed to God, reminding Him (actually, reminding himself) of His power, His sovereignty, and His promises, admitting the people's desperate need for Him. The king cried out, "We do not know what to do, but we look to You" (v. 12). Begg paraphrased the prayer by saying, "Lord, we're just a bunch of pathetic losers. And if You don't help us, we're sunk!"

If you can admit that you're a pathetic loser, then you're well on your way to being desperate for God to move in your heart and life. Do you need to die to self and surrender the reins to the Lord?

CHAPTER 6

GOD USES CRACKED POTS
Jeremiah

God will never come to his right unless we are totally reduced to nothing, so that it may be clearly seen that all that is laudable in us comes from elsewhere.
—**John Calvin**

So I went down to the potter's house, and there he was, working away at the wheel. But the jar that he was making from the clay became flawed in the potter's hand, so he made it into another jar, as it seemed right for him to do.
—**Jeremiah 18:3–4**

WHEN YOU TALK ABOUT BROKENNESS, there is probably no subject or principle in God's Word that is more neglected or misunderstood. As you read the Scriptures, you see men and women of God who were used greatly and at the same time were greatly broken. God often allows setbacks, suffering, and times when we are crushed or broken to reveal to us our desperate need for Him. If we want to be used greatly, we will go through some tough times.

In his book *Lord, Break Me!*, William MacDonald begins by saying, "Usually when something is broken, its value declines or disappears altogether. Broken dishes, broken bottles, broken mirrors are generally scrapped. Even a crack in furniture or a tear in cloth greatly reduces its resale value. But it isn't that way in the spiritual realm. God puts a premium on broken things—especially broken people."[1]

I have two labrador retrievers. Since day one, the black lab, Roxie, has been a compliant dog. I think she's grateful because we saved her when an uncaring owner abandoned her at a convenience store. Since the day we brought her home, she has been loving and easy to train.

Stella, the yellow lab, is a few years younger. She is lovable but strong willed. She chews anything and everything: she dug up termite traps that were buried in the ground, she dug a two-foot hole around a sprinkler head, and she dug up a fifteen-foot drain pipe that was buried a foot deep. Stella chews up limbs, pinecones, toys, plastic, and a variety of other objects never intended to be digested. There is nothing she will not try. She is lovable but not compliant.

After trying everything I knew to do, I asked a friend in the church to take the dogs and train them. After a few weeks he called us over to his house. They weren't the same dogs. Both had learned to be compliant, to heel, to sit (and stay), no matter what. We constantly work with them now to make sure they don't forget who's the boss. As he said to me, "When they get away from me and go back to your house, they will think they are back in charge again. You'll have to show them you are serious—that you are the alpha male and they are just dogs." Now we can walk them without being dragged down the street. They have been, if you will, broken.

You also see this played out with horses. James talks about how the bit controls the head of the horse. By nature a horse will buck if you try to put a saddle or bridle on it. It has to be broken. A horse is an incredible animal, but left to itself, it will be a wild creature. It is useless to the rancher until it is broken. After the horse is taken through the painful and long process of breaking, there is meaning and purpose for its life.

God allows seasons of brokenness to make us totally dependent on Christ. He works to rein us in. While the world applauds the self-made man, God applauds the selfless man. Things gained must be counted as loss. It is God's plan to use times of brokenness to break our pride, not our spirit. If we are going to boast, we need to boast in the Lord and Him alone.

Did you ever play with Play-Doh when you were growing up? You could take it out of the can and ooze it between your fingers. You could manipulate it, mold it, tear it apart, pound it in with other colors, and make all kinds of shapes with it. But if you left the Play-Doh out of the can, it would dry out and you'd have to throw it away. Play-Doh, if left to itself, becomes stiff, inflexible, and useless.

As I get older, I find my body can't do what it used to do. My joints ache, my back aches, and it's harder to get over an injury. I take medicine to keep my joints loose, but the wear and tear of life still stiffens the body. I once could play thirty-six holes of golf and get going the next day with little problem, but now I can hardly get out of bed. If it weren't for a therapeutic massage and a chiropractic adjustment every now and then, I'd be stiff as a board.

The same thing can happen to us spiritually. We can become fixed in our ways and settle into a comfortable holding pattern. Left to ourselves, we can dry up spiritually. We can become hard to the Word and resistant to the hand of the Spirit working in our lives. We can find ourselves sitting in church, inflexible to the call of the cross and insensitive to the prompting of the Holy Spirit.

In the New Testament, we find Jesus' harshest words reserved for the stiff legalists of His day. He rebuked the Pharisees, Sadducees, and scribes for being inflexible, arrogant, and self-righteous. Maybe that's one reason Jesus loved the children; they are flexible. He was attracted to the sick and lame because they knew they needed a physician. He ministered to the prostitutes and tax collectors because they understood their need of forgiveness. Religious, self-sufficient people never know they need to be desperate. Jesus is looking for people who are pliable.

The apostle Paul was proud of his heritage, his religious zeal, and his persecution of the church. In Acts 9 he was confronted and struck down by the Lord. His whole attitude changed and his life was altered forever. The proud persecutor became the humble defender of the faith. He went from boasting about his pedigree to boasting in the cross. Paul could echo the words of John Oxenham's poem, "God's Handwriting":

> He writes in characters too grand
> For our short sight to understand;
> We catch but broken strokes, and try
> To fathom all the mystery
> Of withered hopes, of death, of life,
> The endless war, the useless strife—
> But there, with larger, clearer sight,
> We shall see this—His way was right.[2]

MEN OF CLAY

Jeremiah was the weeping prophet, a man whose heart was broken over his nation. The people of God had drifted away from their allegiance to Jehovah. But while visiting the potter's house, Jeremiah received insight from the Lord into how He works with His people. Although Israel constantly resisted the plans and purposes of God, there was still within them the possibility of usefulness.

> This is the word that came to Jeremiah from the
> LORD: "Go down at once to the potter's house;

there I will reveal My words to you." So I went down to the potter's house, and there he was, working away at the wheel. But the jar that he was making from the clay became flawed in the potter's hand, so he made it into another jar, as it seemed right for him to do.

The word of the LORD came to me: "House of Israel, can I not treat you as this potter treats his clay?"—this is the LORD's declaration. "Just like clay in the potter's hand, so are you in My hand, house of Israel." (Jer. 18:1–6)

Little has changed in the art of pottery through the centuries. It was and still is an art form controlled by the skillful hands of the potter. Though modern technology has improved technique and execution of this craft, it is still the artisan who makes a brilliant masterpiece out of a lump of clay. These craftsmen see what others may not see as they expertly shape and mold this lifeless mud into a work of art.

In the potter's hand, Jeremiah saw a lump of clay. The clay had no meaning, no worth, no value . . . apart from the design in the mind of the potter. The potter takes the lump of clay and slaps it on the board, working out the bubbles—any obstacles or lumps of clay that might be resistant—then begins to put his hand to the process. The wheel starts spinning. The potter works the clay inside out until the vessel he has in mind begins to emerge. He takes something worthless and makes it into a usable vessel, "as it seemed right for him to do."

Clearly the clay is seen as man, the wheel can be seen as the events and circumstances of life, and the potter is the Lord. The wheel is incidental; the key to the illustration is the potter and the clay. Isaiah 64:8 reminds us, "Yet LORD, You are our Father; we are the clay, and You are our potter; we all are the work of Your hands." It is the height of arrogance to think we are the masters of our fate or the captains of our ships and that we can chart any course we want as believers while God sits back and does nothing. He is committed to forming us into the image of Christ. It is imperative that we recognize the hand of God working out the kinks in our lives. We must learn to let the potter do His work without resistance.

WE MUST LEARN TO LET THE POTTER DO HIS WORK WITHOUT RESISTANCE.

If we complain about the times when God is molding us, we are in fact questioning the love and motives of the potter. Isaiah says, "Woe to the one who argues with his Maker" (45:9). We don't need a change in circumstances; we need to change our attitude *about* our circumstances. Believers have no room in their vocabulary for words like *luck*, *fate*, or *misfortune*. We are children of the King, not of chance.

I live in South Georgia where red clay is everywhere. If there's a bald spot in my yard, it's red clay. But I am used to the rich, black dirt of Mississippi where I grew up. Our first full-time position in a church was on the staff of a church in Oklahoma, and we bought our first house there. There was no yard, so we had to plant grass in the heat of summer. I borrowed a tiller from a friend and started to work. The ground was like concrete and refused to yield to the tiller. The resistance of the soil to the blade was so strong that my arms seemed to shake for weeks. We never could get the soil to break up more than one or two inches below the surface.

Left alone, clay will never be anything but clay. Clay is so common, it's worthless. Nobody goes to the local nursery to get topsoil made of clay. No one uses clay in their flower pots. Clay can never be anything but clay—unless someone works it! Our lives have to be worked for there to be fruit that remains. Our heavenly Potter has a design in mind. He has an image to be formed in us. He wants to handcraft us with love.

The late G. Campbell Morgan wrote of Jeremiah 18, "How we have trembled in the presence of those words. The potter molds the clay as he pleases, and the clay cannot object. It has no right to object. That is the doctrine of absolute sovereignty. It cannot fail to make the heart tremble. . . . If there were nothing but the figure of the potter with its awe-inspiring revelation of sovereignty, I should be broken and crushed with hopelessness, but there is more. There is the declaration of the ultimate activity of sovereignty, 'he made it again.'"[3]

REMADE IN HIS IMAGE

There is, in reality, a greater gulf between the potter and the clay than there is between God and man. The clay is not crafted in the image of the potter, but man is crafted in the image of God. With clay, all that is required is the potter's plan. With man, the heavenly Father expects positive cooperation.

We are to be responsive to His slightest touch.

While the potter works, he sees the vessel is flawed. Maybe there is a small stone in the clay or some foreign substance has marred the surface of the vessel. The good news is that the potter doesn't throw it away. He doesn't take it to the flea market and put it on the damaged goods table. It's not marked down for clearance. There is still value in the vessel.

At the potter's house, Jeremiah reminds us that the craftsman remade it. God takes the old clay and starts working it to make it into a new and usable vessel. While we tend to throw away broken vases and call them junk, God throws away the unbroken items and calls them useless. It's our willingness to be broken and remade that allows us to fully experience all God has for us.

The flaw that was found was not the work of the potter; it was found by the potter and revealed by His work. The Lord is committed to remaking us. Sometimes He has to work on us in the area of some secret sin. God points out the flaws and the traps. With our heavenly Potter, nothing is off limits. When we resist, He just works harder and with more intensity. His plan and purpose will not be denied.

Is there currently a flaw in your life that is keeping you from being all the potter has planned for you? Is there an attitude of pride that sees no need for humility? Is there a resistant spirit that finds submission offensive? Is there an affection that has attached itself to you that, left unchecked, could bring you down? Or are you desperate for the potter to remake you so that you can be a vessel He can put on display?

Vance Havner, a prophetic voice of the twentieth century, said, "When I was a boy my father used to take me to an old-fashioned mill by a stream whose waters flowed onto a big waterwheel that turned all the other wheels in the mill. If the miller should discover some morning that the creek had become clogged or diverted so that there was not enough water to operate the mill, he could go up the creek and clear the channel, remove whatever blocked the water's flow, and then he would be in business again. . . . We need to go up the creek, get sin out of our lives, and remove hindrances and debris. Then the Spirit would flow, the wheels would turn, and we would have something to show for our grinding."[4]

The vessel in Jeremiah's prophecy was marred, but it was in the hand of the potter, so there was still hope for it. The potter didn't quit. God has taken vessels just like you and me—marred and flawed as we are—and used us in great and mighty ways. "He made it into another jar," a useful vessel. God is not finished with you. He does not view failure as final.

> **THE VESSEL WAS MARRED, BUT IT WAS IN THE HAND OF THE POTTER, SO THERE WAS STILL HOPE FOR IT.**

My mom had a bookmark in her Bible that was made of silk woven together with the Twenty-third Psalm on it. The front was artistic, but the back looked like a bunch of mangled threads with no purpose or intent. One side was clear and stated truth that brings hope. The other side seemed meaningless. We often tend to focus on the flawed and tangled threads. But God focuses on the beautiful tapestry He is weaving, making our lives into walking witnesses of His divine plan and purpose.

Paul wrote about God's sovereignty in Romans 8:

> We know that all things work together for the good of those who love God: those who are called according to His purpose. For those He foreknew He also predestined to be conformed to the image of His Son, so that He would be the firstborn among many brothers. And those He predestined, He also called; and those He called, He also justified; and those He justified, He also glorified. What then are we to say about these things? If God is for us, who is against us? (vv. 28–31)

In his exposition on Romans, Donald Grey Barnhouse wrote the following words:

> Anyone who gives really serious attention to the Bible must come to the conclusion that God is working all things out according to His eternal plan. . . . God is perfect in His power—He is omnipotent. God is perfect in His wisdom—He is omniscient. God is eternal in His being—He has always known all things and has always been able to do all things. God is the Creator—"All things were made by him,

and without him was not any thing made that was made" (John 1:3 KJV).

The plan of God is centered in the glory of God, the glory of Christ, and the glory of the elect whom He chose before the foundation of the world. We can readily understand that anything God would do He would have to do for His own glory because of His perfectness. Therefore His plan must center in the perfections of His own being and in the perfections which He wishes to bring to us. Nothing can touch us until it has passed through the will of God. "No weapon that is formed against thee shall prosper" (Isa. 54:17 KJV). God has a plan for my life. God is working according to a fixed, eternal purpose.[5]

What we might see as marring, God sees as an opportunity to form us into His image. What we may see as problems are in fact possibilities for God to work in us. God uses all things to build godly character in His children. The foot on the pedal of the potter's wheel and the hands that mold the clay are nail-scarred. The face of the potter is filled with love. We don't have to fear His methods or His motives because He has our best interest in mind.

But if the potter's work is to be permanent, the vessel must go through the fire. In the fire the vessel is strengthened and made useful. Some of the greatest moments of our lives turn out to be the times when we are broken, molded, and reshaped by the Lord. Painful times cause us to cry out to God, and there we find Him, sitting, working, molding, and making us into His likeness.

CHAPTER 7

THE CRISIS OF DESPERATION
Matthew 14

God does not witness to the world by taking his people out of suffering, but rather by demonstrating his grace through them in the midst of pain.
—C. Samuel Storms

He renews my life; He leads me along the right paths for His name's sake. Even when I go through the darkest valley, I fear no danger, for You are with me; Your rod and Your staff—they comfort me.
—Psalm 23:3–4

IN EARLY 2008 I was in Nashville at a screening of *Fireproof*. While I was there, I met a young man, Jon, who shared his story with me about how our second movie, *Facing the Giants*, had impacted his life. As we talked, he began to cry . . . then I began to cry.

Jon and his wife had faced an enormous giant. They had walked through a time of desperation and, in the midst of it, had seen the hand of God. I've asked him for permission to share and summarize his story here.

In 2006 Jon was in Cuba on a mission trip while his wife, Jodi, was at home in Nashville. Emotions had been running high in their marriage for some time, primarily in light of their longtime struggle to have children. Four years into their infertility, they had decided to begin the process of adoption. At the time of the mission trip, they had been pursuing this alternative for about one year. Jodi's heart was raw from the strain, the waiting, and all the related complexities.

Jon said, "It seemed like every day during that mission trip, I ended up visiting with someone who was pregnant," a constant reminder of his and Jodi's struggle to have kids of their own. "While there, a dedicated local pastor was my ministry partner and translator. After I returned home, this pastor friend wrote and suggested that we watch the movie *Facing the Giants*. I had heard of it, but I had not seen the film. Several months passed, and I still didn't take time to sit down and watch the movie. Days turned into weeks, and weeks turned into months."

On July 11, 2007, Jon and Jodi were in Knoxville for the transfer of three embryos they had obtained through embryo adoption. They were told that Jodi needed to rest for twenty-four hours after the transfer procedure. So after the procedure, they found themselves alone in a hotel room far from home with nothing to do but watch movies. A friend had loaned them some DVDs for the trip, and one of them was *Facing the Giants*.

God spoke to this couple through the movie in a profound way. They had already turned their situation over to the Lord, but the film was further confirmation of their total trust in God for the outcome of the embryo adoption. Doctors transferred three embryos but told Jon and Jodi there was only a 25 to 40 percent chance of a single pregnancy from the procedure. Still they turned to the Lord and put each of those embryos in the hands of God, trusting Him for the outcome and praying fervently for each one.

When the movie was over, Jon and Jodi heard the sound of fireworks outside their hotel room. It seemed the timing was orchestrated perfectly in sync with the end of the movie. The fireworks had a special meaning for the couple. They were engaged on the Fourth of July during a fireworks show, and they have always seen fireworks as something symbolic of their love for one another.

Jon said, "Why does it amaze me that the God of the universe could arrange a fireworks display on July 11 just to show us He loves us? Why does it amaze me that a friend in Cuba could get me to watch *Facing the Giants* when I had managed to miss it for months on end despite all the promotion in the United States?"

When they returned home, the couple continued to trust the Lord and wait for the results. When it was time for the ultrasound, it revealed not one, not two, but three little hearts beating away inside Jodi's womb. God had beaten the odds. He had done, as He often does, exceedingly and abundantly beyond what they could have hoped for or imagined. Can you fathom the emotions of that day? They moved from years of crying and desperation to tears of joy and laughter over three hearts beating in the womb.

When Jon and Jodi started trying to have children in 2001, they had no way of knowing that the very same year, these three children would be conceived through another couple's IVF treatments. The entire time they were longing for children, those children were being preserved for them.

I realize that embryo transplant may not be the path for all or even most parents who struggle with infertility. But desperation should lead all of us to the Lord for divine direction. God is sovereign and good. He meets us at the point of our desperation.

The triplets were born on February 2, 2008. Jon and Jodi gave their son the middle name Isaac as a reminder of how God filled their hearts with joy and laughter when they learned they were to receive a triple blessing. Jon and Jodi's three miracles are Ginger Ann, Aaron Isaac, and Sarah Rose.

I have a picture of those three embryos the morning of the transfer, as well as a picture of the triplets at one month of age. Jon first showed me these pictures the day we spoke. I must say, even though we had never met before, the joy of Jesus and the awareness of how God meets us in our crisis of desperation was all over Jon. I felt an instant connection with him. I saw a brother who had walked through an emotional crisis and was still able to shine with the joy of Jesus. The pictures of those three babies reminds me: God always has the last word, even when it seems there is no word, no hope, or no solution to our desperate situation.

NOTHING BUT TROUBLE

If you live long enough in this fallen world, you know that crises will come. Having been born in the 1950s, I've lived through times of upheaval. It seems we are now a society that lives life upside down—what used to be wrong is now thought to be right.

In my lifetime I've lived through the Cuban missile crisis, the revolution of the 1960s, the Civil Rights movement, the Vietnam War, Watergate, double-digit inflation, the televangelist scandals, the child abuse crimes in the Catholic Church, numerous school shootings, 9/11, and a host of other crisis moments. Top that off with personal crises and times when I found myself in desperate situations.

Terri and I struggled for six years to have children. Much like Jon and Jodi, we explored then finally entered the adoption process. Sadly the baby girl we were planning to adopt was aborted at six months. We were devastated. Shortly after hearing that horrible news, we received good news. After six years of tests, frustration, and prayer, Terri was pregnant with our first daughter, Erin.

As I wrote in my book *Prepare for Rain*, another major crisis occurred in my late thirties when I learned of my *own* adoption. This unexpected revelation caused me to deal with deep feelings of anger, deception, and confusion. But there have been many other crisis times, both before and since. In college, I was fired from a church for quoting Martin Luther King in an article. In more recent years, I've helped my dad make the difficult decision to forego life support for my mom. In all these moments, I've found myself desperate for God to give me grace, wisdom, and understanding.

I've watched friends die slow and painful deaths. I've sat at a hospital bedside and watched my father take his last breath, desperate, panicked, and gasping for air. I've asked God, "Why?" when godly men whom I loved dearly have died with so much ministry ahead of them.

While writing this book, a dear pastor friend, Forrest Pollock, was killed in a plane crash along with his teenaged son. He was a leader in our denomination and a friend who often wrote me just to tell me he was praying for me. He was only forty-four—too young in my opinion to be taken. Today his widow, Dawn, and their five remaining children must piece together their lives without a husband and father, and a thriving church must find a way to grieve the loss of its pastor. Life is not a simple formula.

As a pastor, I've had to walk with church members as they faced family crises including suicide, adultery, addictions, pornography, homosexuality, divorce, abuse, and prodigal children. I've seen the ugly side of life. I'm not a counselor, but I have seen the beauty of grace when many have walked through the stench of life. In those crises I've seen some people blossom in their faith while I've seen others curse God.

Vance Havner and his wife, Sara, had no children. They married late in life and often traveled together. One day in the early 1970s, Sara was struck with a serious and painful illness. Out of that painful crisis, Vance Havner wrote *Though I Walk Through the Valley,* one of the greatest books on suffering and grief I've ever read. In the preface he talks about how "grief and sorrow and bereavement have been my bedfellows, and what I once knew only by observation I know now by experience. Only those who have traveled this road really know what the journey is like."[1]

CRISIS MOMENTS ARE DEFINING MOMENTS. THEY MAKE US OR BREAK US. THEY REVEAL WHERE WE PLACE OUR TRUST.

I remember visiting Dr. Havner one day at a hotel in Spartanburg, South Carolina. While there, he let me read a letter, now tattered and worn, that he carried in his wallet. It was a letter his beloved wife had written him years before. It spoke of her love for him and her belief in the calling of God on his life. He told me how much the mere reading of that letter encouraged him when he was alone in a hotel room. Dr. Havner wondered what the future would hold. He had no children and he was alone. But he was not really alone; he had the Lord, and he prayed that he would make it home before dark. He prayed that this crisis and loss would not cause him to stumble in his faith journey.

Crisis moments are defining moments. They make us or break us. They reveal where we place our trust. Whether it's a health crisis, a church crisis, or a family crisis, we find out what people are made of when a crisis comes.

It seems that if there's not a crisis, the media will create one. Their news reporting is driven by crisis situations. They tend to ignore good news and focus on disasters. A local newspaper once told my daughter, "We don't report plane landings, just plane crashes." Every day the media tells us of some catastrophe somewhere in the world.

- Violent crime
- Natural disasters
- Collapse of savings and loan
- Major denomination ordains homosexuals
- Two students open fire in school, killing eight
- Food shortages, poverty, and world hunger
- High divorce rates in the church
- Scandals in Congress
- Rising gas prices
- Mortgage crisis
- Identity theft
- Terrorism

What makes it worse is we now know about crises and catastrophes we would have never heard about a hundred years ago. Before the rise of technology and communication, we wouldn't hear about murder, rape, flooding, or starvation in other parts of the world. Now we get instant information about every problem imaginable. It's enough to make you want to stay in bed and pull the covers over your head.

There are times when our faith is tested and we go through the crisis of belief. There is no such thing as a saint without a trial or a trial without the presence and provision of God. Watchman Nee said, "To hold onto the plow while wiping our tears, that is Christianity."[2]

ENDURANCE IS IN THE DETAILS

It is well known that the Chinese symbol for the word *crisis* represents both opportunity and danger. Pain and suffering may bring danger, but they also bring an opportunity for maturity and growth. Dr. Karl Slaikeu and Steve Lawhead describe a crisis as "a bomb that explodes in your life and shatters it. More specifically, a crisis is a state of extreme emotional upset that is touched off by some hazardous event."[3]

Crisis can be created by good and bad events in our lives. Some crises come because of our changing times. Technology has led our children to be savvy in ways we never dreamed. About the time we figure out how to turn on the car stereo, they've sent seventy-four text messages. Kids understand how to maneuver around the Internet better than we do. This has created incredible opportunities and unimaginable evil.

One of the breakthrough technological inventions of our time is the iPod. I have enough storage space on my iPod not only for music but also for full-length movies and television shows. Right now I have about five thousand songs on a device that can fit in my shirt pocket. It blows me away that the computers we used to put men into space were the size of a house and didn't have one-tenth the capacity of my handheld iPod. That means technology is good, right?

Maybe.

What about those who use their iPods to listen to music that demeans women or certain races? What happens to people who never take the plugs out of their ears long enough to hear the truth? Their minds are loaded with stuff from the pit.

Ron Dunn preached a sermon in which he made a very profound statement that I've never forgotten: "Good and evil run on parallel tracks, and they normally arrive about the same time." With blessings come battles. While we are immersed in new technologies and improved safety features, we sometimes fear for our lives. These are dangerous times. We can put men on the moon and launch rockets into space to send back pictures from Saturn, but we can't make the average city safe to walk in at night.

WE CANNOT LET THE FOLKS WHOSE MOTTO IS "YOU CAN'T DO THAT" RUN OUR LIVES.

We live in nicer homes than our parents ever dreamed of, but are we better off? My grandparents never locked their doors. I have motion detectors, smoke alarms, and a home security system. Yet I still think about rising crime rates and home intrusions. There are senior adults in our church who won't come to church on Sunday nights because they don't want to go into their homes after dark. They are fearful and, can't we admit, rightfully so.

Part of the key to surviving a crisis is perseverance. We must keep getting up and going about our business as normally as possible. I remember President Bush urging Americans to get back to "normal" as soon as possible after 9/11. Why? Because he didn't want the country to be paralyzed by fear. He wanted our country to send a message to the world—especially to our enemies—that fear and terrorism would not dominate our lives. We would move forward, and we would survive.

The reason many believers fail during times of testing, crisis, and desperation is because they aren't willing to push through to God. They give up. They resign themselves to a "less-than" existence. They see no hope or future. All they can see is doom and gloom, and they can't bring themselves to believe the truth of Romans 8:28—"We know that all things work together for the good of those who love God: those who are called according to His purpose."

We need to keep our hands to the plow and our eyes on Christ. This world is not our home. Our circumstances do not have the last word. This fallen world and human depravity must not determine our outlook. We cannot let the folks whose motto is "You can't do that" run our lives.

Has your crisis led you to the point of giving up? Are you listening to the naysayers, or to the Lord God of heaven? Are you willing to trust God and take Him at His Word? History records countless stories of those who have persevered when everyone around them said they should give up. When you stop living and believing, you start dying.

PROFILES IN PERSEVERANCE

I have numerous biographies of Winston Churchill in my library. I am fascinated by the man. It is hard for me to imagine how he could have been defeated as prime minister of Great Britain after leading the country to victory in World War II. If it had not been for Churchill's bulldog tenacity, the English might be speaking German today.

When he was defeated, his wife said it could be "a blessing in disguise." Churchill responded, "If it is, then it is very effectively disguised."[4] Churchill was not finished. He continued to be a viable part of England's political landscape and served his country in immeasurable ways. What if he had given up? What if he had retired and spent the rest of his life painting? What if he had decided he wouldn't write anymore or step up if called to serve again?

Think about the following people who kept pressing on. Not all are believers, obviously, but all remind us that it's always too soon to quit.

- Dr. Seuss's first book was rejected by twenty-three publishers. When he finally found a publisher, his first book alone sold six million copies.
- Vince Lombardi didn't become a head coach in the NFL until he was forty-seven, and now the Super Bowl trophy is named after him.
- During their first year of business, Coca-Cola only sold four hundred Cokes.
- During the depression, Bobby Jones and Clifford Roberts

had trouble getting anyone to join the Augusta National Golf Club. They tried to sell houses and build a subdivision around the course to help pay for it.

- In his first three years in the automobile business, Henry Ford went bankrupt twice.
- Michelangelo spent seven years lying on his back to paint the Sistine Chapel.
- After years of unsuccessful experiments, imprisonment for debt, and ridicule from family and friends, Charles Goodyear finally developed a type of rubber that would not be affected by temperature extremes.
- NBA great Michael Jordan was cut from his high school basketball team.
- Archie Manning's dad committed suicide, and Archie was the one who found him dead. He almost gave up football at Ole Miss.
- In 1905 the University of Bern rejected Albert Einstein's Ph.D. dissertation.
- Abraham Lincoln failed at most of his attempts in business and politics.
- John Bunyan wrote *The Pilgrim's Progress* during a long stay in prison.
- The official church rejected Martin Luther.
- John Knox is buried under a parking lot.
- Joseph made it to Pharaoh's palace by way of both the pit and prison.
- Moses experienced forty years in the desert before he led God's people out of Egypt.

- David ran for his life for years before finally becoming king of Israel.
- Jeremiah was the weeping prophet.
- The apostle Paul had enough scars to make any man want to quit.
- Today the church is growing in Muslim countries despite incredible opposition and persecution. While American Christianity seems to be declining, the persecuted church is prospering.

A crisis can bring incredible opportunity. It is often in the crisis that we find Christ in a new and significant way. For those of us who know Christ, the storm is an opportunity to see the Lord afresh. Think about that stormy night on the Sea of Galilee recorded in Matthew 14:

> Immediately He made the disciples get into the boat and go ahead of Him to the other side, while He dismissed the crowds. After dismissing the crowds, He went up on the mountain by Himself to pray. When evening came, He was there alone. But the boat was already over a mile from land, battered by the waves, because the wind was against them. Around three in the morning, He came toward them walking on the sea. When the disciples saw Him walking on the sea, they were terrified. "It's a ghost!" they said, and cried out in fear.

Immediately Jesus spoke to them, "Have courage! It is I. Don't be afraid."

"Lord, if it's You," Peter answered Him, "command me to come to You on the water."

"Come!" He said. And climbing out of the boat, Peter started walking on the water and came toward Jesus. But when he saw the strength of the wind, he was afraid. And beginning to sink he cried out, "Lord, save me!" Immediately Jesus reached out His hand, caught hold of him, and said to him, "You of little faith, why did you doubt?" When they got into the boat, the wind ceased. Then those in the boat worshiped Him and said, "Truly You are the Son of God!" (vv. 22–33)

I love this story. It's one of my favorite passages. Here you find a time when fear and faith collided. The disciples heard the messages; they listened intently to the Sermon on the Mount; they had just heard the parable of the sower, the seed, and the soil; they witnessed the feeding of the five thousand. They were riding high, but in a matter of hours their faith would be stretched. In an instant the disciples moved from the lecture to the lab where Jesus would test their faith. Would they, in a crisis, believe God or would they panic?

Because of the geography of that region, storms can come up suddenly. This was not a light breeze with a little chop; this was a severe storm. It was strong enough to rattle even the most experienced fishermen. In absolute darkness the winds howled and the waves crashed over the sides of their small fishing vessel. The prospects of survival didn't look good.

But there was someone with them in the storm. At the time when all hope seemed lost, when the crisis seemed too much, Jesus came walking to them on the water. At first they thought He was a ghost. But when we walk by faith, we see Jesus in the storm.

I love the way George Duncan describes this moment: "If panic had already begun to seize the minds of the fishermen; if fear lest the storm would overwhelm their tossing craft had already laid its cold hand upon the hearts of these men; if turbulence marked the scene upon which they gazed, then, in staggering and amazing contrast, peace and serenity seemed to rest upon that kingly form as it moved towards them out of the night."[5]

AT FIRST THEY THOUGHT HE WAS A GHOST. BUT WHEN WE WALK BY FAITH, WE SEE JESUS IN THE STORM.

It seems that only Peter had learned anything from Jesus' sermons and miracles. While the others were holding on for dear life, Peter asked if he could come to Jesus. Practically speaking, of course, this was an impossible request. But when Jesus is in sight, the impossible becomes a Him-possible. While the other disciples probably sounded like Job's friends, rebuking Peter for his foolishness, Peter had a focused faith. Despite the circumstances and crisis, he called out to Jesus, "Let me come to you on the water." Jesus said, "Come." Simple. Direct. To the point.

Maybe you picked up this book because you are in the midst of a storm. You may be in a desperate situation, feeling hopeless and helpless. It may be the waves of circumstances are crashing in on you and you feel yourself starting to sink. But remember, it's safer on the water with Jesus than in the boat without Him.

I've got good news for you. You are right where God wants you. You are on the verge of believing God in a new way. Your faith is about to expand. If you will press through to Jesus, if you will step out of the boat and act in faith according to His Word, you could join the ranks of those who have learned to find God in their crisis.

Your story is about to change.

If you will continue on this journey with me, I believe that at the end, God will use His Word, His Spirit, and maybe a few truths from this book to show you the power of desperation.

CHAPTER 8

WHEN THERE'S NOWHERE ELSE TO TURN

Mark 5

There can be no hope without faith in Christ, for hope is rooted in him alone. Faith without hope would, by itself, be empty and futile.
—Ernst Hoffmann

Why am I so depressed? Why this turmoil within me? Put your hope in God, for I will still praise Him, my Savior and my God. . . . The LORD will send His faithful love by day; His song will be with me in the night—a prayer to the God of my life.
—Psalm 42:5, 8

I FIRST MET John and Kathleen Hemken in the early 1990s. John had just transferred here to Albany, Georgia, with a major corporation, and he brought with him an incredibly talented wife and great kids. John was a blessing to me as a layman and then served as executive pastor for a number of years. He took a great load off me, especially in difficult and stressful times.

His wife, Kathleen, was very involved in our women's and music ministries. She sang on our praise team and was one of our featured soloists. Her passion for Christ was always evident when she sang. She and John were also very involved in bringing leadership to our intercessory prayer ministry.

During their time here, Kathleen began to have health issues. After numerous trips to the doctors, they diagnosed her with a serious and life-threatening condition that demanded immediate and aggressive action. I've asked Kathleen to share her story with you.

> I was diagnosed with multiple endocrine neoplasia II in the fall of 1996 and had my first surgery in October of that year. Three of my four parathyroid glands were removed because they contained bad tumors. Through additional testing, more tumors were found in my pancreas and liver, and I went back to surgery on February 19, 1997. The doctors at Emory informed us of the procedure and also said that if the tumors had spread into the lymph system, they would not be able to cure me. They found

many more tumors in my pancreas and liver, and they had indeed spread into the lymph system. They just sewed me back up and gave us the bad news. The doctors said there was very little chance I would be around in five years, but they wouldn't start chemo because I was not on the downhill slide yet.

I remember feeling like I had been hit by a truck, and I was overwhelmed with questions. When and how would I tell my children? It was a very dark and difficult time for us. I went downhill physically, emotionally, and spiritually very quickly. I was dealing with a lot of pain and would finally drift off to sleep and then wake up thinking, "Is this really real?" But then there was that black cloud of reality waiting for me. In addition, I battled terrible feelings of loneliness. Where was God? I felt despair and fear—some for myself because I knew the worst case at hand, but mostly for John and the kids since they would be left behind while I was safely with Jesus. I was uncertain about what they would do. The pit closing in on me seemed very deep and very dark and very real.

My friend Marty Estes came to stay with me and give John a break on Sunday, February 23, 1997. She asked what she could do, and

I said, "I don't know, just pray." And she did. Marty came again on Monday, and she taped a poster of Isaiah 53:5 to the wall of my room, reminding me that "by His stripes" I was healed. I told Marty I was at the bottom emotionally and couldn't even pray for myself. She said, "Kathleen, that's why so many people are praying for you." She put on some praise music. I just laid there with my eyes closed and thought, "Jesus, You are the only way out of this!"

At that very moment, the Lord Himself came and talked to me, two feet in front of my face. He said, "Kathleen, if you can believe Me and trust Me for your salvation, you can believe Me and trust Me to heal you. Now I am going to heal you. This isn't going to be a doctor thing or a Kathleen thing; this is going to be a Jesus thing. Just like you didn't do anything to earn your salvation, you also didn't do anything to earn this healing. This is something I am choosing to do. All you have to do is take the prayers of the saints out of My hand and you can have this. You feel like you are in a pit. I know how you feel. You have one stripe. How many do I have?"

God also spoke to me about some other things in my life. He told me I had a "have" and "have not" attitude in how I talked about

Him with others. I could talk about Him to my friends with all kinds of ease, but I did not do the same with my lost family members. I knew exactly what He was talking about with respect to my family. I have reflected many times on these moments and realize God wants total obedience, not just what is convenient or help-ful at the time.

This short but life-changing experience concluded with the Lord saying, "Now you go around and tell people what I've done for you. I'm making this all brand new for you, so don't waste it!" After that conversation He was gone. Immediately the pain and nausea went away. I sat up in bed and started yapping my head off. Praise God!

The Lord confirmed my healing in many ways through Scripture He had given to me and to many others. However, I had to walk it out by faith for more than a year before there was any medical "proof." I've had the chance to share with doctors who have acknowledged this could have only been a "Jesus thing." God is who He says He is. He is not a liar. He does what He says He will do. Here I am eleven years later in 2008. I never had chemo, and I am doing great with a clean slate of health. Our family is blessed beyond belief, and we are all very grateful. To God be all the glory—great things He has done!

MEDICAL MISERIES

Kathleen's story is similar to one we find in Scripture. The woman with the issue of blood had exhausted all her options. Doctors couldn't cure her, and the advice of friends had not helped her. She was a desperate woman with an incurable problem, but desperation led her to seek the Lord. In doing so, this unnamed woman of the first century received something that doctors could not explain. She exercised faith when all seemed hopeless. She reached out to touch the hem of Jesus' garment and found deliverance in her moment of desperation.

This miracle, recorded in Matthew 9, Mark 5, and Luke 8, has been called by commentators a miracle within a miracle—a parenthetical miracle. The shame, pain, and desperation of this woman is seen clearly. "A woman suffering from bleeding for 12 years had endured much under many doctors. She had spent everything she had and was not helped at all. On the contrary, she became worse" (Mark 5:25–26). What a picture of helplessness and hopelessness.

I love what John Laidlaw wrote about this miracle: "It was a cure obtained without a word spoken beforehand."[1] Spurgeon called it "a wayside miracle." Apparently the Lord had never met this woman, and she had never met Him. But in a divine moment, deliverance took place. This miracle happened while Jesus was on his way to heal Jairus's daughter. Jairus was a man of prominence; this woman was an outcast. God would heal and deliver in both situations because He is no respecter of persons.

One thing we must understand when we are desperate is that the resources and power of God never run dry. He is not taxed, drained, or overworked by the needs of the hour. In fact, our desperation is an opportunity for God to prove Himself as the all-sufficient One.

Something stirred the heart of this woman. She had tried everything and had been everywhere. She had sought out every legitimate doctor, every quack, and every proclaimed healer in the land, but the flow of blood could not be stopped.

According to Levitical law, as an unclean woman she would be prohibited from going to the synagogue or the temple for worship.

> When a woman has a discharge of her blood for many days, though it is not the time of her menstruation, or if she has a discharge beyond her period, she will be unclean all the days of her unclean discharge, as she is during the days of her menstruation. Any bed she lies on during the days of her discharge will be like her bed during menstrual impurity; any furniture she sits on will be unclean as in her menstrual period. Everyone who touches them will be unclean; he must wash his clothes and bathe with water, and he will remain unclean until evening. When she is cured of her discharge,

she is to count seven days, and after that she will be clean. (Lev. 15:25–28)

As a woman in the first century, her only options were to be a wife and work around the house. Her condition would have made it impossible for marital intimacy and, thus, for child bearing. Imagine the pain and loneliness of this life. Excluded from relationships with friends and family, unable to have visitors at her sickbed, she had nowhere to turn. She was as much an outcast as a leper was. She probably had some so-called friends, like Job's, who told her the condition was because of some hidden, unconfessed sin.

Probably because of the ignorance of the times, she was also one whom other women sought to avoid, in case her condition was somehow contagious. Here we find a woman who was drained physically, an outcast socially, and bankrupt financially. The picture was bleak. The future looked dark. There seemed to be no hope.

> **MAYBE HER FAITH WAS THE SIZE OF A MUSTARD SEED OR EVEN SMALLER, BUT SHE GOT UP AND STARTED MAKING HER WAY TO JESUS.**

Everywhere she went, there was embarrassing evidence of her presence. For twelve long, exhausting, and expensive years she had suffered. She had spent everything, depleted her resources, and was no better for the effort, no closer to the cure.

Most of us would have given up. Many would say, "What's the use? I've tried it all. I've spoken to the experts. I've seen my charts. There's no hope. There's no cure. I'll just lie down and die." Certainly she wasn't the only woman in Galilee with this problem. But she's the only one we know of who went to Jesus for a cure. She's the one who sought Him out; therefore, her story has been recorded for eternity.

She had done all she could, but now she knew something supernatural had to be done. It couldn't wait. This was really a last gasp effort. Maybe her faith was the size of a mustard seed or even smaller, but she got up and started making her way to Jesus.

Perhaps she recalled hearing the story of the four lepers recorded in 2 Kings 7. Their future looked hopeless and their options were exhausted. They finally turned to each other and said something to this effect: "Why are we sitting here until we die? We're going to die anyway, so we might as well get a meal in our bellies first. What are they going to do, kill us? We're dead already."

If they stayed where they were, they would starve to death. If they went into the city, they would starve. If they went into the camp of the Arameans, they could be killed, but at least it would be over and done with. They must have reasoned, "If death is all we have in our future, it's probably better to die quickly than to sit here and die a slow, painful death of starvation."

Research and statistics tell us that starvation is a slow and horrible death. "Complete starvation in adults leads to death within eight to twelve weeks. In the final stages of starvation, adult humans experience a variety of neurological and psychiatric symptoms, including hallucinations and convulsions, as well as severe muscle pain and disturbances in heart rhythm."[2] Eighty-five percent of starvation deaths occur in children five years old and younger. One person dies from starvation every 2.43 seconds.[3]

You've seen the images. Kids with nothing but skin and bones, bloated bellies, flies all around their faces. They would give anything to have the food we throw away on a daily basis. We know nothing of hunger. We say, "I'm starving," but we don't have a clue. We've never been desperate for food. These lepers were. They got up and made their way toward the camp. What they found there was deliverance in the form of delicacies.

WHEN DESPERATION MEETS FAITH

Maybe you've bought the devil's lie to sit around and throw yourself a pity party. "Why don't I just sit here and die? Nobody cares. Nobody even knows how low I am. What difference would it make if I were dead or alive?" Then maybe this book has found its way into your hands to encourage you to get up and find God, to get up and get going by faith.

It's not enough just to be desperate.

Desperate people take overdoses and commit suicide. Desperate people do foolish things. But desperation married to faith leads to a different solution. This woman believed God could change her situation.

It's possible she had not been at this point before. Perhaps she had sought counsel from the Pharisees, thinking her religious leaders might be able to give her some kind of help. But they wouldn't want to associate with unclean people who might spoil their Sunday clothes. Perhaps the self-righteous Pharisee condemned her and gave her no hope. It's possible she had talked to someone with lousy theology who told her God didn't care about people. Regardless, she had given up on the world's solutions and came to the Savior.

In *The Miracles of Jesus*, Leslie Flynn writes, "The Talmud lists at least eleven cures for this trouble, then common in Palestine. Though some astringents likely proved helpful in stanching the flow of blood, other remedies were such superstitious acts as carrying the ashes of an ostrich egg in a linen bag in summer and in a cotton rag in winter. To get rid of this debilitating sickness, she had tried every imaginable cure but without success. She was a 'perpetual menstruant.'"[4]

If she were living in our day, she might have bought the lie that some television faith healer was the answer to her problem. She could have spent all she had, planting her "seed faith" gift, only to discover the healer had no power to heal. Something inside stirred her heart to make one more effort. A small grain of faith started to grow in her heart. Maybe, just maybe, Jesus would be different from the Pharisees, charlatans, and con artists who had offered their "assistance."

Let's learn something from this brave woman. Look at the different accounts in Scripture:

"for she said to herself . . ." (Matt. 9:21)

"Having heard about Jesus . . . she said . . ." (Mark 5:27–28).

She was down but not out. She was despairing but not without a glimmer of hope. A small seed of faith was taking root in her heart. Clovis Chappell writes, "Here is a woman who is having a conversation with herself. We all do that at times, and what we say to ourselves is vastly important. Of course, we recognize how tremendously we are influenced by the words of others. A wrong word has often meant the utter marring of a life. Many a child foolishly rebuked for stupidity, for instance, by a parent or teacher has gone out under that influence to a lifelong battle with an inferiority complex. . . . There is, in fact, no measuring the possible harm of one wrong word."[5]

We're not talking about self-help or pop psychology here. This is the power of words. Who do we listen to? What do we say to ourselves and about ourselves when we are alone? Do you beat yourself up, or do you seek to see yourself as a child of God, redeemed by the blood of the Lamb? The Word of God speaks of the power of words. The wisest man who ever lived gave us Proverbs related to how we speak and who we listen to.

> The words of the wicked are a deadly ambush,
> but the speech of the upright rescues them.
> (Prov. 12:6)

> Stay away from a foolish man; you will gain no
> knowledge from his speech. (Prov. 14:7)

> Pleasant words are a honeycomb; sweet to the
> taste and health to the body. (Prov. 16:24)

The words of a man's mouth are deep waters,
a flowing river, a fountain of wisdom.
(Prov. 18:4)

Listen closely, pay attention to the words of the
wise, and apply your mind to my knowledge.
(Prov. 22:17)

In times of desperation, I would encourage you to dig into the Word. Listen to the Word. Study it, meditate on it, memorize it. Fill your mind with thoughts from the mind of God. If you listen to the wrong people, you learn the wrong lessons. If you don't allow God to teach you in your desperation, you will be a defeated disciple. How have you been thinking about your situation?

WHAT DO WE SAY TO OURSELVES AND ABOUT OURSELVES WHEN WE ARE ALONE?

- "The doctors have given me no hope. I quit. I will lie here and die."
- "My finances are a disaster. I'll never get out of debt. I think I'll go out to eat and put it on my credit card."
- "Everything I do, everywhere I turn, it's bad news."
- "The doctors have told us we could never have children."
- "No one really cares about what's going on with me. I think I'll just drop out of my Sunday school class. They won't even notice I'm gone."

The devil applauds this kind of thinking. I would call it "stinking thinking." It's certainly not thinking with the mind of faith. It's not a believing, overcoming attitude. It fails the "ask, seek, and knock" test. It is devoid of "If any man is thirsty, let him come to Me" seeking.

Some of us are like Alexander and his "terrible, horrible, no good, very bad day." Remember the kid who woke up with gum in his hair and decided he should move to Australia? His siblings found cool prizes in their cereal boxes while Alexander just found cereal. But his bad day was just beginning. The misery continued as Alexander's terrible day included a trip to the dentist, lima beans for supper, and kissing on television.[6] Sometimes we're like Alexander, wallowing in misery when the Lord wants us to get desperate.

ACTION PLANS

I heard a preacher long ago talk about what to do in times of trouble. He said, "Throw a party." I'm not sure any of us feel like having a party when we are in despair, but I know none of us have trouble throwing a pity party, whether with friends or all alone. We must push through our natural inclinations and start believing God as never before. If we stay where we are, we will die in our hopelessness and despair. But as long as there is breath, there is the capacity for hope and faith. This is not wishful thinking; this is knowing that my God can supply all my needs.

The woman in Luke 8 decided to take one final risk. Getting up off the bed was an act of faith. Pushing through the crowd was an act of faith. Risking humiliation and heckling by the crowds as they saw her bloody clothes was an act of faith to get to Jesus, no matter what others said.

I'm sure the devil whispered in her ear every step of the way. "You can't be serious. This will never work. What makes you think anything will be different this time? You are just going to make a fool out of yourself. Aren't you embarrassed enough without putting yourself through this?" Be honest, the reason we don't get up and press through the crowd to get to Jesus is simple: pride. We worry about public opinion and what others will think of us. Until we get past that, we aren't really desperate.

I heard Vance Havner preach on this passage in the 1970s. He said, "Desperation is not enough; she had faith. She believed that if she could just get through to Jesus and touch the hem of His garment she would be healed. Many were thronging Him that day, but she touched Him. Her touch was different. It may have been an imperfect touch, an imperfect faith, but it is not the quality or quantity of faith that matters in the end. It is the *object* of faith. She pressed through the crowd and touched the hem of His garment."

Scripture reveals that somewhere, somehow, she had heard about Jesus. "Having heard about Jesus, she came behind Him in the crowd and touched His robe" (Mark 5:27). Upon hearing, she acted. When Jesus healed Peter's mother-in-law, the Bible records that the news spread.

In that day and time, communication was slow. Today it would be impossible for us to comprehend how slowly the news traveled, but it did spread. They didn't have telegraphs, telephones, the Internet, or text messaging. There was no evening news or regional newspaper. But the word got around.

It traveled down the dusty roads. It traveled from one side of the Sea of Galilee to the other. It traveled through the shepherd's fields, the leper colonies, the small villages, and the cities. The word was out: Jesus of Nazareth is healing the sick, the lame, the lepers, and the blind. Maybe she had heard of Him even healing on the Sabbath. She could have thought, "Anything is possible. If them, why not me?"

Look at her spirit of dependence and desperation: "If I can just touch His robes, I'll be made well!" (Mark 5:28). As David Redding noted, "While Jesus was in a race with death for that little girl (Jairus's daughter), a nobody interrupted him."[7] That nobody became a somebody because Jesus noticed.

"Instantly her flow of blood ceased, and she sensed in her body that she was cured of her affliction. At once Jesus realized in Himself that power had gone out from him. He turned around in the crowd and said, 'Who touched My robes?'" (vv. 29–30).

Please note the phrases "instantly" and "at once" in this passage. The miracle was immediate, and immediately Jesus responded. The Gospel accounts of Matthew and Luke are specific that it was the fringe or the sacred tassel that she touched. It would have been a tassel she could have touched while coming up behind him. One thing is obvious, she wasn't trying to make a scene or draw attention to herself.

I love what Redding says here, "Christ had 'presence,' and

everything was so right with Him that it affected whatever was wrong with anyone else."[8] She felt an immediate change in her body. Her condition changed in the same moment Jesus felt power go out of Him.

Jesus turned and asked what sounds like a dumb question, but God never asks dumb questions. He was probing and looking for a confession. He wasn't looking to rebuke her but to reward her. His response was different from anyone she had known in the past twelve years. Others in the past ran to wash themselves of her uncleanness, but Jesus stopped and engaged her in a conversation.

Of course, the disciples didn't get the question. "His disciples said to Him, 'You see the crowd pressing against you, and You say, 'Who touched Me?'" (v. 31). This woman's touch was different than the swarming of the rest of the crowd. Some were starstruck. He was a celebrity riding a wave of popularity. The crowd was curious, but she was desperate. The masses had decided to check out this miracle worker. She was determined to touch His garment and go her way. Jesus wouldn't let that happen.

A TOUCHING ENDING

It's easy to come to church, fellowship with believers, and never touch Jesus. We can be in the crowd and never really be part of the congregation. We can sing songs but never worship. We can take notes on sermons, and never apply the Word to our hearts. Attendance doesn't mean we're paying attention. I believe Jesus is passing by the aisles of our churches every Sunday, looking for people who are desperate for Him. Unfortunately most of us miss Him because we aren't really desperate to worship and adore the Lord of glory.

When Kathleen encountered God in her hospital bed, she touched Jesus. She wasn't content for her faith to be overwhelmed by her fears. She recognized that Jesus was her only hope, and He met her at the point of her desperation.

Jesus issued a public plea to the woman with the issue of blood. It was probably the last thing this frail, exhausted woman wanted or expected. Others had demanded money for their cures. Jesus sought only a confession. "He was looking around to see who had done this. Then the woman, knowing what had happened to her, came with fear and trembling, fell down before him, and told Him the whole truth. 'Daughter,' He said to her, 'your faith has made you well. Go in peace and be free from your affliction'" (vv. 32–34).

Here was the only good news she had heard in twelve long years. Not only was she healed, but her faith was affirmed and she was given a command: "Go in peace." Peace. Something so far removed from her experience, she thought she would never have it again. Yet here was the Prince of Peace offering her what no one else could. Peace of mind. Peace in her soul. Peace in her tormented body. Peace in her heart.

Desperate people look for peace. Some look in the wrong places. Some look for peace in the bottom of a shot glass. Others look for peace in medications and drugs. These things numb the body, but they do not bring peace. People think they can find peace in earthly relationships. Peace only comes through

Christ. There is no lasting peace outside the One who has said, "Go in peace" (Mark 5:34), "Peace, be still" (Mark 4:39 NKJV), and "My peace I give to you" (John 14:27). He alone gives the peace that passes all understanding, the peace that will guard our hearts and lives (see Phil. 4:7). Those of you who are desperate, push through the throngs and touch the Prince of Peace.

Turn to Jesus; He will turn to you!

CHAPTER 9

WHEN YOU ARE UP AGAINST THE IMPOSSIBLE
Mark 9:14–29

Unbelief makes the world a moral desert, where no divine footsteps are heard, where no angels ascend and descend, where no living hand adorns the fields, feeds the birds of heaven, or regulates events.
—F. W. Krummacher

Then Jesus said to him, "'If You can?' Everything is possible to the one who believes." Immediately the father of the boy cried out, "I do believe! Help my unbelief."
—Mark 9:23–24

IN THE VATICAN GALLERY hangs Raphael's last painting, which some think to be his greatest masterpiece. It is entitled *The Transfiguration*. The uppermost part pictures the transfigured form of Jesus, with Moses on the left and Elijah on his right. On the next level down are the three disciples—Peter, James, and John—recently awakened and shielding their eyes from Jesus' blinding brilliance. Then on the ground level is a poor demon possessed boy, his mouth hideously gaping with wild ravings. At his side is his desperate father. Surrounding them are the rest of the disciples, some of whom are pointing upward to the glowing figure of Christ, who will be the boy's only answer. Raphael has brilliantly captured something of the overwhelming contrast between the glorious Mount of Transfiguration and the troubled world waiting below.[1]

Mark 9:14–29 is a picture of the world in which we live. It is a world of contrasts. On one hand, we know the love, grace, and power of God. On the other, we find ourselves facing seemingly impossible situations where we feel totally helpless. At some point along life's journey, we all come to the crossroads of faith and fear. We stand at the intersection of hope and despair, and we have a decision to make. Will we choose to believe God and His Word, or will we collapse in despair, doubt, and fear?

The life of George Mueller is an incredible story of faith. Here was a man who faced daily impossibilities yet daily experienced God's adequacy. Mueller's story is one of God's faithfulness. At every turn, regardless of the need, it seemed there was always God's provision just in time. Mueller said that all this was possible in answer to believing prayer.

Rarely do I find myself facing difficulties with the attitude of Mueller. More often I am like the disciples, taunted, mocked, and ridiculed by others for their lack of power. Faced with a demon possessed boy, they did not know what to do or how to respond.

Jesus along with Peter, James, and John were returning from the Mount of Transfiguration. God had revealed Himself in a breathtaking, awe-inspiring way. Then the appearance of Jesus changed from the inside out, and the disciples got a glimpse of His glory. It was so incredible that Peter wanted to build a campsite there and hang out on that mountain for the rest of his life, basking in the glory of the moment. The problem is that we disciples aren't made to live on mountaintops. We are made for valleys. We are called to intersect with humanity in all its shortcomings.

AND NOW FOR SOMETHING COMPLETELY DIFFERENT

Meanwhile down at ground level, far from the mountaintop experience their friends were enjoying, the other nine disciples were not having so great a time:

> When they came to the disciples, they saw a large crowd around them and scribes disputing with them. All of a sudden, when the whole crowd saw Him, they were amazed and ran to greet Him. Then He asked them, "What are you arguing with them about?"

THE POWER OF DESPERATION

Out of the crowd, one man answered Him, "Teacher, I brought my son to You. He has a spirit that makes him unable to speak. Wherever it seizes him, it throws him down, and he foams at the mouth, grinds his teeth, and becomes rigid. So I asked your disciples to drive it out, but they couldn't." (Mark 9:14–18)

The cynics and skeptics were having a heyday with the other nine disciples. The scribes were taunting them and verbally abusing them, mocking the disciples and, in reality, the Lord as well. The disciples failed attempt to cast out the demon had started a heated discussion.

In Mark 3 we read that Jesus had appointed the twelve apostles "to be with Him, to send them out to preach, and to have authority to drive out demons" (vv. 14–15). In Mark 6 we find these words: "He summoned the Twelve and began to send them out in pairs and gave them authority over unclean spirits" (v. 7). If the disciples had authority going out two-by-two, there should have been no problem for nine dealing with one boy.

Note the word "amazed" in verse 15. The word means to be astonished or frightened. A. T. Robertson's insight helps us understand the word: "The sudden and opportune appearance of Jesus in the midst of the dispute when no one was looking for him turned all eyes to him. He would not fail, however the disciples might do so. The people were awed for the moment and then running began to welcome him."[2]

Are you amazed when Jesus shows up in your moment of

need? Why are we frightened to seek Him? Why do we fail to search for Him? Others may fail us, but Jesus never fails. He is not a distant deity who is unfamiliar or uncaring about our life issues. He cares and He comes when we call.

BETWEEN DOUBT AND DESPERATION

The story of this young man is a sad one. Luke's account of this story tells us this was the man's only son. Imagine the heart-break and frustration of seeing your only son in such torment. Jesus quickly recognized what was happening and put Himself in the middle of the situation and conversation.

The difference between this man and the average person in need is that this man was willing to be honest. He didn't gloss over the problem. He didn't try to explain it away. He didn't seek to look good at all costs. Public opinion no longer mattered; others' feelings were secondary. He was a desperate father who had come to Jesus and His disciples, hoping that something might change.

The father had probably already gone through all the advice of the scribes and Pharisees. Perhaps he was now a social outcast, shunned by those in the community who feared his son. Little children would be pulled inside when this possessed boy walked the streets. Satan had, for all practical purposes, destroyed this man and his son.

The picture that the Bible paints of this boy is one that Hollywood would love to use for special effects. But this was not a stunt; it was real life. The young son was foaming at the mouth, deaf and dumb, his body uncontrollably slammed to the ground, thrown into the fire and then into water. The scars must have been dreadful. The bruises must have been deep purple all over his body. The boy's form was being destroyed incident-by-incident, moment-by-moment, day-by-day. Even the unconditional love of his father couldn't bring the boy back. He was at the end of his rope. This young man had reached the point of impossibility.

Now he was in a position to see God work.

Maybe your situation is nowhere near the extent of this one, but you are defeated nonetheless. Satan uses you like a punching bag. Just about the time you think you've got your act together, he karate chops you and knocks you to the ground. You feel beaten, battered, and bruised. Emotionally you don't know if you can take it anymore; mentally it's draining the life out of you; spiritually you wonder if God even cares.

You may find yourself listening to the wrong people. It is evident in God's Word that the crowd was no help to this man or his son. The crowd is fickle and can't be trusted. They will cheer you one minute and banish you the next. Listening to the crowd can be a dangerous thing.

Or maybe you have been disappointed by God's people, by the church, or by a minister. The nine disciples were unable to help. It wasn't a lack of desire that hindered the nine; it was a lack of faith. God's people will disappoint you because they are frail flesh just like you are. God's servants aren't perfect. If your desperation leads you to curse the church or the servants of God, it's because you've put your faith and hope in men and institutions rather than in the Lord God of heaven.

Note the response of our Lord in verse 19: "You unbelieving generation! How long will I be with you? How long must I put up with you? Bring him to Me." Can't you hear Jesus saying this to His disciples even today? Can't you hear that rebuke being given to the church of the twenty-first century? I can. We are, by and large, a pitiful model to this desperate world of the power of the gospel. I'm not talking about healing as much as I am about Holy Spirit power and believing faith. We lack power and faith. We fail God at basic points of discipleship. We can no more sidestep the Lord's diagnosis and frustration than those first-century disciples could.

WE CLAIM TO HAVE THE ANSWERS, YET WE OFTEN DON'T EVEN KNOW THE QUESTIONS.

"How long?" had to be a statement of frustration. Jesus certainly knew His time on earth was drawing to a close. Would the disciples ever get it? Would they ever apply what they had learned and live it out consistently?

In a world going to hell, dominated by darkness, depravity, and destruction, the church stands silent and impotent. We appear to have nothing to offer those who are desperate. The problem is not in the power of Christ. The problem is the prayerlessness and powerlessness of the church. We claim to have the answers, yet we often don't even know the questions.

Someone has said that knowing these disciples had been authorized with power to cast out demons yet could not do it caused this man to doubt if the power was even available. Maybe they followed the formula they had previously used in casting out demons. They had, in fact, cast out demons in the past, but this time the disciples failed. Too often the world comes to the door of the church looking for deliverance, and they find us having theological debates and tea parties.

I heard Jerry Vines say in a sermon, "We are so compromised and so powerless in the face of the onslaughts of this world and so helpless before the media . . . no wonder the lost world walks by our churches, snubs their noses, and says, 'They can't do it, they haven't got any power.'"

Read carefully these words by A. W. Tozer. He hits the nail on the head as to the problem in the average church when faced with the basic issues of life.

> The present position of Christ in the gospel churches may be likened to that of a king in a limited, constitutional monarchy. The king . . . is in such a country no more than a traditional rallying point, a pleasant symbol of unity and loyalty much like a flag or a national anthem. He is lauded, feted, and supported, but his real authority is small. Nominally he is head over all, but in every crisis someone else makes the decisions. On formal occasions he appears in his royal attire to deliver the tame, colorless speech put into his mouth by the real rulers of the country.
>
> Among the gospel churches Christ is now in fact little more than a beloved symbol. "All

Hail the Power of Jesus Name" is the church's national anthem and the cross is her official flag, but in the week-by-week services of the church and the day-by-day conduct of her members, someone else, not Christ, makes the decisions.[3]

Let's be honest with ourselves. The average church doesn't want Jesus to be there. We don't want the kind of people that Jesus attracted: sinners, prostitutes, the demon-possessed, tax collectors, outcasts of society. We like to sit in our nice, neat circles in our folding chairs, having our little theological discussions about everything from predestination to who will care for all the pets left behind at the rapture. Are we not, in fact and in practice, an unbelieving generation? We hear stories of power in other places around the world, but where is the power of God in the American church? Where's the church that is doing things that cannot be explained apart from the infusion of Holy Spirit power in the life and breath of the body of Christ?

Jesus tells them to do what we must do as well. "Bring him to Me!" Whatever the situation, take it to Jesus. No issue is too great, no need too small for Jesus. Take your family, your prodigal, your broken marriage, your desperate situation to the Savior. Throw yourself at His mercy, and seek Him while He may be found.

HELP MY UNBELIEF

Let's continue the story from Mark 9:

So they brought him to Him. When the spirit saw Him, it immediately convulsed the boy. He fell to the ground and rolled around, foaming at the mouth. "How long has this been happening to him?" Jesus asked his father.

"From childhood," he said. "And many times it has thrown him into fire or water to destroy him. But if You can do anything, have compassion on us and help us."

Then Jesus said to him, "'If You can?' Everything is possible to the one who believes." Immediately the father of the boy cried out, "I do believe! Help my unbelief."

When Jesus saw that a crowd was rapidly coming together, He rebuked the unclean spirit, saying to it, "You mute and deaf spirit, I command you: come out of him and never enter him again!" Then it came out, shrieking and convulsing him violently. The boy became like a corpse, so that many said, "He's dead." But Jesus, taking him by the hand, raised him, and he stood up.

After He went into a house, His disciples asked Him privately, "Why couldn't we drive it out?" And He told them, "This kind can come out by nothing but prayer and fasting." (vv. 20–29)

I love the late Ivor Powell's commentary on this section: "That disappointed, harassed parent did not reiterate all the condemnatory remarks concerning the helpless disciples; he did not elaborate on the disappointing results of his earlier request. He brought his problem child to Jesus. Other people in a similar situation might have remained at home allowing their molehill of disappointment to become a mountain of bitterness. This man seemed to have practiced the old adage, 'If at first you don't succeed, try, try again.' He ceased looking at the helpless disciples and focused his attention on the Lord."[4]

As you read this story in the other Gospels, you discover facts about this father and son you don't need to miss:

- He was his only son. (Luke 9:38)
- The father got on his knees and humbled himself before the Lord. (Matt. 17:14)
- The demons seemed to have control of the boy to do as they wished. (Mark 9:18)
- The boy would scream uncontrollably. (Luke 9:39)
- The demons had a heyday with the boy, abusing him mentally and physically. (Mark 9:18)

If you listen to some folks talk about the Lord, you can come to a couple of conclusions. Either they don't know what they're talking about (meaning, they've obviously never read the Bible or they've read it out of context), or they live in denial of the power of the Holy Spirit, failing to believe that the Spirit's work is the Lord's work. They never seem to make the connection between the words of Jesus regarding the promise of the Spirit and the power received by those who follow Christ.

Others appear to communicate that God loves some people more than others. This simply is not true, based on Scripture. God does not grade on a curve, though many seem to believe so. God does not play favorites. He searches for those who will seek Him with all their heart, soul, mind, and strength.

Finally, some believe that trials and tests are not of God, even though we see repeatedly in Scripture how God uses tests and trials to define and refine His children. Sometimes we can see more through our tears than we can through a telescope.

I don't believe in pat answers to serious problems or in formulas for faith. One reason Jesus didn't heal people the same way every time is because we would have taken His one method and formed an entire theology around it. As an old preacher once said, "We would have had the one-spit crowd, the go-dip crowd, and the touch-the-hem crowd." People who live their lives by formulas instead of faith are often in error but rarely in doubt. Could it be the nine disciples had tried to use an old formula and weren't meeting a current situation by seeking fresh power from on high?

> SOMETIMES WE CAN SEE MORE THROUGH OUR TEARS THAN WE CAN THROUGH A TELESCOPE.

Suffering is a reality. Suffering will not end in this lifetime. It is not the *lack* of suffering but knowing what to *do* with your suffering—that's the key. Richard Baxter wrote, "Suffering so unbolts the door of the heart that the Word hath easier entrance."[5] Faith is tested in times of suffering. In the refining fires of life, we find what we are made of and who or what we are trusting. Robert Murray McCheyne summarized it this way: "A dark hour makes Jesus bright."[6]

The man brought his son to Jesus—good decision. Jesus called this father to stand up and believe. Doubt has a way of grasping our throats and choking us. None of us are immune to it. The great preacher C. H. Spurgeon said on one occasion, "My peculiar temptation has been constant unbelief. I know that God's promise is true. Yet does this temptation incessantly assail me."[7]

Think about it and be honest. Do you believe God can do anything? Really? Do you believe God will do what He says in His Word? Now let's be honest. We believe, but we need help with our unbelief. We have a hard time believing the words to the old song, "What He's done for others, He'll do for you."

This man stands before Jesus and hears the Son of God challenge him to believe. Jesus didn't tell him to wish it into existence or hope that he could get to a place where all his dreams could come true. He called the man to belief. I read a great quote by an anonymous author on biblical faith: "Anything that goes beyond the Word of God is not biblical faith. It is something else assuming its appearance." Jesus called to this man and told him that the condition for his son's deliverance was faith.

The man's response seems a little uncertain and somewhat skeptical. He wasn't sure he could step out that far. "If You can do anything . . . " Let's try translating his statement a little: "I'm here, but I'm not yet *all* here. I'm not totally sure. I came here believing there was a possibility, but was it just wishful think-ing? The lack of ability I saw in Your disciples threw me for a loop."

Jesus asked him what the problem was, not because Jesus needed this vital information to diagnose it but because the father needed to verbalize and communicate the depth of his desperation. This father's statement was his final declaration of desperation. His hope was slipping away, but at least he was honest. Too often our response quivers with doubt, but we try to cover it up with high-sounding spiritual language to keep it from sounding unspiritual. Honesty brought the father into a position where Jesus could stretch his faith.

Look again at the father's initial response: "If You can do anything . . . " Jesus gave him a rebuke of sorts. "What do you mean by saying, 'If I can'? I'm not the issue here. I can do any-thing. The ball is in *your* court. Everything is possible for him who believes." A. E. J. Rawlinson reminds us that those who have faith "will set no limits to the power of God."[8]

MIRACLE WHIPLASH

There is an element of some religious talk that abuses a verse like this. Some play the "name it and claim it" game. They see God as a gofer or a butler who stands at our beck and call to do whatever we want. This passage is often taken out of context by television preachers, faith healers, and others who imply that you can get whatever you want merely by daring to ask for it, merely by forming the words with your lips. It is not biblical to dictate your demands to God. It is erroneous to believe that if you work up enough faith, God is obligated to act according to your whims. That's not faith; that's arrogant presumption.

I don't see a demon under every rock, nor do I believe that a miracle a day keeps the devil away. At the same time, I've seen God do the miraculous. I believe God still wants to do that which cannot be explained. I believe in healing; I just don't put my faith in faith healers. I believe God can do the miraculous; I don't believe miracles ceased sometime after the apostles died. However, I don't believe we can have miracles on demand.

It is important not to limit the Holy One. Even a quick glance at the Gospel of Mark reveals the power of Christ to intervene in the physical realm:

HONESTY BROUGHT THE FATHER INTO A POSITION WHERE JESUS COULD STRETCH HIS FAITH.

- The demoniac in the synagogue in Capernaum (1:23–27)
- Peter's mother-in-law (1:30)
- The leper (1:40–45)
- The paralytic (2:1–12)
- The man with the withered hand (3:1–6)
- The calming of the storm (4:35–41)
- The Gadarene demoniac (5:1–20)
- The woman with the issue of blood (5:25–34)
- Jairus's daughter (5:21–24, 35–43)
- Feeding the five thousand (6:31–44)
- Walking on the water (6:45–52)

- The daughter of the Syrophoenician woman (7:24–30)
- The deaf and dumb man (7:31–37)
- Feeding the four thousand (8:1–9)
- The blind man (8:22–26)
- The demon possessed boy (9:14–29)
- Blind Bartimaeus (10:46–52)
- The withered fig tree (11:12–14, 20–25)

Eighteen miracles appear in this shortest gospel. The late Greek scholar A. T. Robertson wrote, "If one takes out of Mark's Gospel all the miracles wrought by Jesus and every mention of the miraculous or the supernatural, he will have only a mutilated fragment. When the miraculous is removed, only a bare skeleton remains. In most of the reports, action and authentic word are so closely interwoven that it is impossible to separate them. . . . We should be constrained to believe what we cannot explain. . . . We must constantly keep in mind that God has laws unknown to us. They operate regardless of our ignorance of them."[9]

I believe God can do anything, but I don't believe God has to do whatever I want Him to do. I've prayed for people to be healed; some have and some haven't. I've watched godly, faithful prayer warriors suffer greatly. Surely they of all people could find deliverance. Certainly their problem wasn't a lack of faith. This much I know: if your faith means you can figure God's ways out, your faith is greater than anyone's in the Bible. His ways are not our ways. This doesn't mean we should sit in quiet resignation and defeat. We should bring our concerns, our fears, and our cares to the One who can change our circumstances according to His will, confident that Jesus will respond. The question is not "What can Jesus do?" but "What am I willing to trust Him for?" When He says, "All things are possible to him who believes," He's not giving us a blank check to ask whatever we want, whenever we want it. The Creator is the One who sustains, and the One who sustains also delivers. The greatest deliverance is from the grasp and power of sin and Satan. Any other deliverance is secondary to His redemptive deliverance.

In times of desperation, this father's statement may best summarize the anguish of our souls. "I do believe! Help my unbelief." Oswald Chambers wrote, "If we would only get into the way of bringing our limitations before God and telling Him He cannot do these things, we should begin to see the awful wickedness of unbelief, and why our Lord was so vigorously against it. . . . Unbelief is the most active thing on earth. . . . Unbelief is a fretful, worrying, questioning . . . self-centered spirit. To believe is to stop all this and let God work."[10]

ALL OVER BUT THE SHOUTING

Don't miss this other important aspect of what the man said. He did not say, "Lord, you need to help me believe." He said to Jesus, "Help my unbelief." The battle often rages when we are called on to trust the Lord in a new dimension of faith. The Word made flesh called out for faith in this man. The father admitted his doubt and pleaded in desperation for God to help him get beyond his doubts and fears. Jesus then turned to the son and dealt with the issue. Alexander MacLaren said, "Jesus does not lecture us into faith, he blesses us into it." Ron Dunn, preaching on this passage, said, "Jesus performed the miracle that would help the man's unbelief. He took the situation in hand. There are times when the Lord rebukes the poverty of faith by the abundance of His grace."

After Jesus challenged the man's faith and healed the boy, it looked as if things were moving from bad to worse. It appeared the demons might win the day. No chance. "But Jesus, taking him by the hand, raised him, and he stood up" (Mark 9:27). It was their one last effort to control this poor boy. But Satan is a defeated foe. Jesus had not called the man out to embarrass him or to watch him walk away further frustrated. No, He called him out so the glory and power of God might be revealed. The cynical scribes, the taunting crowd, and the disillusioned disciples would have no doubts about the power of Christ and the defeated, inferior forces of this world.

Everything changed. The man's son was made whole and set free from a lifetime of misery and suffering. The father walked home with a new son that day, and the father himself left a changed man. He had gotten through to Jesus, and Jesus had gotten through to him. Desperation brought the man to Jesus, and he left with delight and deliverance.

When the man and his son left, the disciples, who were probably embarrassed and confused, came to Jesus with their questions. "After He went into a house, His disciples asked Him privately, 'Why couldn't we drive it out?' And He told them, 'This kind can come out by nothing but prayer and fasting'" (vv. 28–29). There are instances in our lives that cannot be fixed by a bandage or an aspirin. In those times we must learn that God has limited Himself in order to drive us to prayer. Anything that makes us pray is always a blessing. Any prayer that casts itself in desperation upon the all-sufficient Savior is always a good thing.

CHAPTER 10

THE DAY OF VISITATION

Mark 10

We can never be blessed until we learn that we can bring nothing to Christ but our need.
—Vance Havner

Rest in God alone, my soul, for my hope comes from Him. He alone is my rock and my salvation, my stronghold; I will not be shaken. My salvation and glory depend on God; my strong rock, my refuge, is in God. Trust in Him at all times, you people; pour out your hearts before Him. God is our refuge.
—Psalm 62:5–8

MY FRIEND TIM SHEPPARD has written a number of great songs over the last few decades. He wrote "Would You Believe" when he was a teenager. He is a master wordsmith. For a long time he dropped out of the music scene to minister to his aging parents, but in 2007 he recorded his first project in years.

One song in particular on Tim's latest album struck me: "I Hear the Lord Passing By." It is based on the story of blind Bartimaeus on the road outside Jericho.

> I hear the Lord passing by,
> This could be my day of visitation.
> Have mercy on me, Lord,
> Hear my cry of desperation.
> I hear the Lord passing by.
>
> My heart, my flesh
> Yearn to be with You.
> Open my eyes to see Your glory
> All the days of my life.[1]

Mark's gospel records the desperate story of Bartimaeus as Jesus passed by on His way out of Jericho.

> They came to Jericho. And as He was leaving Jericho with His disciples and a large crowd, Bartimaeus (the son of Timaeus), a blind beggar, was sitting by the road. When he heard that it was Jesus the Nazarene, he began to

cry out, "Son of David, Jesus, have mercy on
me!" Many people told him to keep quiet, but
he was crying out all the more, "Have mercy
on me, Son of David!" Jesus stopped and said,
"Call him."

So they called the blind man and said to
him, "Have courage! Get up; He's calling for
you." He threw off his coat, jumped up, and
came to Jesus. Then Jesus answered him, "What
do you want Me to do for you?"

"*Rabbouni*," the blind man told him, "I want
to see!"

"Go your way," Jesus told him. "Your faith
has healed you." Immediately he could see and
began to follow Him on the road. (10:46–52)

Jesus was on His way to the cross. This would be the last
time He would pass through Jericho. Beggars lined the dusty
road as they always did. Hoping that someone would give them
a handout or throw them a few coins, they would shake their
cups, rattle their canes, and shout out in despair. The sick were
there. The lame were there. The beggars were there. Picture
the pathetic scene—every beggar wanting something from
someone.

But one beggar stood out on this day. One got the attention
of Christ. This passage has been called "the shout that stopped
God."

Make no mistake—it was a shout of desperation.

But why would Jesus stop for this one—this Bartimaeus? That's exactly what the disciples wanted to know. Some tried to get him to shut up, but he shouted all the more. Others prob-ably told him to calm down, but he couldn't. A few must have thought, *Jesus is a busy man with a busy schedule. If he stops for every blind beggar, He's never going to get to Jerusalem.* So they tried to tell Bartimaeus to be quiet. But they couldn't stop him or shut him up. He was a desperate man. He was a persistent man. Nothing and no one was going to stop him from doing all he could to get the attention of Jesus. For Bartimaeus, it was now or never.

> **ONLY DESPERATE PEOPLE GET TO THE POINT WHERE IT'S NOT ABOUT THEM BUT ABOUT THE LORD.**

Jesus did stop. He heard the cry of this blind beggar. He responded to the shout of desperation. Then He surprisingly asked what seems to be a dumb question: "What do you want Me to do for you?" Think about that. What would a blind beggar possibly want from Jesus?

Let's make this question personal. What do you want Jesus to do for you? Is He a bandage when what you really need is spiritual surgery? Is He nothing more than an ecclesiastical bell-hop that you expect to be available at your beck and call? Is he like jolly old Saint Nick searching for good boys and girls to give toys to?

Why are you desperate?

Do you have a specific answer to that question?

I've met believers who get desperate only when they get

THE DAY OF VISITATION

in a pinch. They make all kinds of promises to God, but when they get out of the bind, they go back to their old ways. Their promises are fleeting. Their interests in the Lord are temporary. They want what God can do for them, but they don't really want *Him*.

If Jesus asked you what you want, would you want the right thing? Is it Him that you want, or merely the gifts from His hand? Mark's gospel records James and John being asked this same question (10:36). They came boldly to Jesus (arrogantly, you might say), demanding that He give them whatever they asked of Him. James and John foolishly asked to sit on His right and left hand in positions of power. Jesus rebuked them, reminding them that greatness and power come from being a servant. James and John had a lot to learn about Jesus and the cross life. Jesus rebuked the attitude that seeks selfish gain.

We live in a time when more and more believers are giving the wrong answers to the questions Jesus is asking. If Jesus were to pass by us and ask, "What do you want Me to do for you?" most of our answers would be self-centered. I would imagine the average believer would say something like:

- I'd like to find the right mate.
- I'd like to get out of debt.
- I'd like to win the lottery.
- I'd like to have a new car.
- I'd like to have a life free from pain and suffering.
- I'd like to own my own company.

Unfortunately most of our answers would have little or nothing to do with the glory of God in our lives. Only desperate people get to the point where it's not about them but about the Lord.

I can read your mind right now. You say, "But Bartimaeus made a selfish request." I'm glad you brought that up.

If you read the story, you find Jesus told him to go on his way, but he followed Jesus. Having been delivered, he chose to be a disciple. He walked out of Jericho with the Lord. Where was Jesus headed? To the cross. I'm convinced God will answer your prayer of desperation if in your answer Jesus is glorified and the cross is magnified.

WHY SO DESPERATE?

Why didn't Jesus heal everyone that day? Why just one? Apparently, Bartimaeus was the only one who was desperate. Others were crying out for healing and alms for the poor. Bartimaeus was crying out for mercy. There's a big difference between wanting God to give you money and wanting God to show you mercy. On the surface it looked like Bartimaeus was no different than the others. He wanted what the others wanted. But Jesus could see into the heart. Jesus heard his heart when all the others just heard his voice.

The question Jesus asked does seem like an odd one coming from the Son of God. He knew, of course, what Bartimaeus wanted. But what Jesus wanted was the honest confession of a desperate man.

Here was a blind man who was begging. There was no

welfare or unemployment office to appeal to, no Salvation Army or homeless shelter where he could find refuge on a cold night. He was helpless and hopeless. Isn't it obvious what a blind man would want from the Great Physician?

Yes.

And no.

Jesus always probes to see if we are desperate for Him or just interested in using Him for what we want. The reality is that many want from Jesus that which He will not give. We come to church, check the box, do the religious thing, and think God owes us our every wish. We make Him out to be like a genie in a bottle, and we want to negotiate for more than three wishes.

In this "I want it all and I want it now" culture, we can easily buy into a gospel of God-on-demand. We can buy the lie that God will make you a leader but never require you to be a servant—greatness without humility, riches without sacrifice. That kind of so-called "faith" might work for a while, but it's not biblical. God never gives to fulfill our flesh. God only answers cries of desperation that bring Him glory. If Jesus gave most of us what we asked for, it would ruin us.

The story of Bartimaeus is a simple but profound story. The Lord asked the same question of Bartimaeus that he did of James and John. With the disciples, he got a selfish request. With the blind man, he got a request that caused him to stop and respond.

Maybe Bartimaeus had heard of other miracles. Possibly a leper had passed by and shared his testimony. Perhaps a traveler on the way to Jerusalem had mentioned the feeding of the five thousand. It's possible that Bartimaeus's memory could have been stirred by these stories and he thought, *What He's done for others, maybe He could do for me.* Bartimaeus wasn't asking for a handout; he wanted Jesus. He didn't want money; he wanted mercy.

BE CAREFUL WHAT YOU ASK FOR

As a minister for nearly forty years, I've met believers who really didn't want Jesus to heal them. Believe it or not, there are some people who enjoy their sickness. It gives them something to whine and complain about. It lets them get sympathy from others. If they were healed of their infirmities, they wouldn't have anything to talk about. Every time you come across them, all they want to talk about is themselves, not about what the Lord can do.

Jesus probed this blind beggar. "Do you really want to be healed? Do you understand the full implications? As bad as it may seem, if I heal you, you're going to have to get up and get a job. You'll have to take responsibility for your life. You'll be expected to stop begging. No more handouts or free rides."

Desperate people are desperate for a reason. They've come to the end of their rope. They are willing to cast aside all obstacles to get to Jesus. They no longer care what others think. They refuse to listen to the crowd because they have moved into a new dimension of desperation that is willing to lay it all on the line.

Unfortunately desperate people sometimes make the wrong choice. They turn to ungodly counsel, or they are tripped up by

Satan and become deceived into thinking there is another path other than the one that leads to the throne of grace.

In the fall of 2007, our church was shaken when one of our members—a husband, father, and businessman—took his life. In an instant this apparently typical Christian family was shattered, left to process this unspeakable tragedy. This man taught young people in Sunday School with his wife and was an active member of the music ministry. Yet there was a side of his life that lacked accountability. This resulted in his choosing the wrong path.

His wife had already walked through her fair share of desperate situations. She watched close friends die young who were taken too soon in our reasoning. Her own sister fought cancer for many years before the Lord took her home. Then her father suffered a stroke that dramatically changed their lives. Though traumatic and painful at the time, she now realizes that God was using all of these situations to prepare her for the unthinkable—her husband's suicide.

We know now that her husband was not the man we believed he was. How often have we discovered duplicity in the Christian community that leads to an intricate web of deception? As life began to unravel, the husband finally confessed his double life to his wife. There was hope that the restoration process would begin and that healing would take place over time. It was not to be.

A few days later this wife and mother pulled into her driveway and was met with the awful news that her husband had taken his life.

Desperation can lead to times of darkness and hopelessness. But in those desperate times, we can find God in the midst of the storm. His grace can be and will be sufficient. Our help does come from the Lord. We don't find sufficient grace in self-help books, inspirational songs, or a pat on the back but from the indwelling Holy Spirit who watches over us and abides in us. God is our source and resource.

If you are going through a desperate time right now, remember that God will give grace for the moment. There is no magic wand. There are no quick answers. Deep hurts won't heal overnight. But the promises of God are new every day. Isaiah 42:16 says, "I will lead the blind by a way they do not know; I will guide them on paths they have not known. I will turn darkness to light in front of them, and rough places into level ground. This is what I will do for them, and I will not forsake them."

Regardless of the desperate situation—physical blindness, the deception of a double life, or the agonizing pain of betrayal and loss—God will not forsake you. Bartimaeus is a reminder that no matter what else you see, if you don't see yourself in desperate need of the Master's touch, then you are blind. God cannot do what He longs to do in your life if you are sitting on the sidelines, unwilling to admit how desperate you really are.

SAY IT LIKE YOU MEAN IT

Bartimaeus cried out. He would simply not be silent. Some believers today are so scared of showing any emotion that they sit on their hands in fear of actually enjoying an experience with the Lord. They are so afraid they might get out on a limb, they won't even climb the tree. Bartimaeus realized his desperate situation and cared little about public opinion or the thoughts of his peers. Vance Havner said, "Notice that some tried to discourage Bartimaeus, and even Christians may discourage earnest seekers, but Jesus can hear the sinner's cry over all the commotion and turmoil."[2]

I was the student minister at Roswell Street Baptist Church in Marietta, Georgia, in the early 1980s. During that time Mark Price signed to play basketball with Georgia Tech. Terri and I loved to watch Mark play. He had a great career at Georgia Tech and was voted into the Tech Hall of Fame in 1991. As a point guard considered by some to be too small and too slow, he was selected first in the second round of the 1986 NBA draft.

Mark played for twelve years in the NBA, spending most of his career with the Cleveland Cavaliers. He was a four-time NBA All-Star. Mark is still the NBA's all-time leader in free throw percentage at 90.4 percent and the Cavaliers' all-time assists leader. During the 1988–89 season Mark was

DEEP HURTS WON'T HEAL OVERNIGHT. BUT THE PROMISES OF GOD ARE NEW EVERY DAY.

only the third player in the NBA to complete 40 percent of his shots from three-point range, 50 percent from the field, and 90 percent from the free throw line. He was a pure shooter.

One day while I was watching Mark at a Georgia Tech game, I thought, *I wish I could have played basketball like Mark. I wish I had been given that kind of talent.* I loved basketball when I was growing up, but I wasn't willing to discipline myself to be that kind of athlete. What I was really thinking was, *I don't want to pay the price to be that kind of player, but if God would choose just to zap me with that ability one day, that would be really nice.* I wasn't willing to pay the price (no pun intended); I just wanted to get the gift.

If I had really wanted to play like that, I would have been willing to sacrifice to make it happen. I would have become a gym rat. I would have readjusted my life to make the effort. Isn't that how we often approach the Christian life? We may want to be an "All-American" in our faith, but if we're only making a Little League commitment to Christ, we can't expect God to respond in the affirmative.

The reality is that while there is an element of desperation needed, we are actually as spiritual as we want to be. If we were passionate about the Lord Jesus, we would make changes in our schedule. We'd stop worrying about people's perception of us. We wouldn't live in fear of our peers. We would cast aside whatever was hindering us in our pursuit of Christ because He is a rewarder of those who diligently seek Him.

When Jesus called Bartimaeus out of the crowd, he threw aside his cloak and ran to Christ. The cloak was the long, flowing outer garment he wore. But in order to get to Jesus, it might cause him to stumble, so the blind man threw it away. It was more important to get to Christ than to keep tabs on his cloak. Bartimaeus didn't wait for the crowd to sing ten verses of "Just As I Am." He jumped up and didn't waste any time.

When Jesus calls us to Himself, He demands that we cast something aside. There is something in our lives that hinders us from following. It may seem insignificant to others, but it is a stumbling block for us. Could it be there's something in your life that is keeping you from getting to Jesus?

CHAPTER 11

GOD MAY SEEM SLOW, BUT HE'S NEVER LATE

John 11

There is many a thing which the world calls disappointment, but there is no such a word in the dictionary of faith. What to others are disappointments are to believers intimations of the way of God.

—John Newton

Therefore He had to be like His brothers in every way, so that He could become a merciful and faithful high priest in service to God, to make propitiation for the sins of the people. For since He Himself was tested and has suffered, He is able to help those who are tested.

—Hebrews 2:17–18

I HAVE A PASTOR FRIEND, Ed Litton, whose wife was tragically killed in an automobile accident—the awful interruption to a day that started like any other but ended in devastating loss. Ed Litton serves as the pastor of the First Baptist Church of North Mobile, Alabama. He is one of the most gifted communicators I've ever met, and First Baptist North is one of the greatest churches I've ever been privileged to preach in. In June 2008, I asked him to preach at the Southern Baptist Convention Pastors' Conference on brokenness. It was one of the most powerful and anointed messages I've ever heard. It was a message delivered from a broken heart by a man who has walked through the deep, dark valley of grief.

The following is the entry Ed wrote in his blog on August 28, 2007, just twelve short days after the home-going of his wife.

> "The length of our days is seventy years—or eighty, if we have the strength; yet their span is but trouble and sorrow, for they quickly pass, and we fly away" (Ps. 90:10 NIV).
>
> One week ago my life changed. In one swift moment the unthinkable became reality.
>
> The afternoon of Thursday, August 16, 2007, I was in another office at the church, meeting with a friend from out of town. My wife, Tammy, and daughter Kayla were traveling after school to Hattiesburg, Mississippi, for Kayla to audition with a cello professor.

An hour or so after they left me at the office, I heard my cell phone ringing on my assistant's desk. I let it ring, thinking Judy would pick it up. Then my private phone began ringing, followed by my cell phone again. Suddenly I remembered Judy had left the office early for an out-of-town trip. Immediately I left the meeting to answer my cell phone.

My precious daughter's voice was on the other end. "Daddy! Oh, Daddy!"

"Kayla, what's wrong?" I asked, as my heart rose to meet my throat.

"Mommy is asleep and a man just pulled me out of the car." I knew what that meant: tragedy had intruded into our everyday existence. Instantly I knew I needed to be with my daughter. The man who pulled Kayla from the wreckage then got on the phone.

"Is my wife OK?" I asked urgently.

"Sir, you need to get down here as soon as possible."

I don't know how, but in approximately thirty minutes Dr. Mike Cook, my longtime friend and colleague, drove me to the halfway point between Mobile and Hattiesburg—the scene of the accident. Traffic was backed up almost a mile. We drove on the shoulder of the road until a policeman directed us to take the opposite lane. An ambulance was parked at the top of a slight hill; Kayla was lying on a stretcher inside. An eighteen-wheeler sat facing west in the right lane a few hundred yards from where our truck stopped. As Mike navigated to the ambulance, I saw a group of men standing around.

As a pastor I've been present at the site of many gut-wrenching situations. I cannot tell you how many times I have been at the scene of horrible traffic accidents, suicides, and other such tragedies. In every case the severity of the tragedy that has just occurred can be readily judged by the manner in which people stand around, awkwardly shuffling their feet with their heads down, avoiding eye contact. As we came upon the scene and I observed those present, I said, "Mike, Tammy is gone!" Though he sought to reassure me that I may have been making a premature estimation, in my heart I knew otherwise.

I stepped into the ambulance to comfort my terrified daughter. At that time we thought Kayla's arm might have been broken. Medical personnel would not tell Kayla or me anything about Tammy. Once assured that Kayla was in good hands, I stepped out into the humid sunshine to go and see about my precious wife.

I was stopped by a medic. I pulled away and continued on my way to her. A patrolman motioned for me to step back because I was standing where the helicopter was about to land. I went back into the ambulance. At this point Kayla was crying for me not to make her fly in the helicopter. I assured her that it was safe and that I would be with her.

Mike and a highway patrolman motioned for my attention. "Mr. Litton, you need to sit down." "No," I said, "shoot straight with me." My dear and courageous friend Mike said, "Pastor, Tammy did not make it. I am so sorry!" I do not know how to express what I felt; it was shock and I knew it was shock. I was numb yet fully aware that what I had just been told was true. The helicopter landed, and a tall medic in a blue flight suit said to me, "Mr. Litton, come this way." He escorted me to the passenger side of the helicopter. The seat belt was trapped and snapped in place. I shook hands with the pilot and thanked him for his help. I heard noise in the back and felt the cabin pressurize as the back door was closed. "Stand by," the pilot announced to the crew. "Ready!" was their response.

As the helicopter lifted upward, I took note of my emotions. No tears yet, no panic, though I wouldn't call it peace. It was peaceful, but it was simply a still moment—the kind of moment God has used in my life many times when He was about to punctuate a truth in me. As we lifted I could see those men—those sweet helpless helpers who had come to my wife and daughter's rescue. They stood awkwardly around Tammy's body, now covered with a blanket. Two men attempted to shield my view of her with a blue tarp. I remember thinking, "Don't do that. It's okay."

As the helicopter lifted up swiftly, I could not take my eyes off of her petite frame lying beneath that blanket. Then suddenly, clearly, the Spirit of God spoke to my shocked and wounded heart. He said, "This is the path Tammy took just a few minutes ago." Peace flooded my soul for the next fifteen minutes as we made our way to the trauma center in Mobile. I knew God had sent His holy angels, and they had lifted her up on wings like eagles. She rose as if raptured into His holy presence.

You may call me a mystic. Perhaps I am, but I believe God graces us with moments of insight. I believe He occasionally allows us to stand so close to the edge that we see His glory and hear the fluttering of angels' wings. I cling not to my experience that day; I cling to the

Word of God by which I judge my experience, and I find nothing inconsistent in my life or in the Second Coming of Christ.

Psalm 90:10 tells us, "The length of our days is seventy years—or eighty, if we have the strength; yet their span is but trouble and sorrow, for they quickly pass, and we fly away." My sweet wife did not get seventy or eighty years in this life. From my earthbound and sorrowful perspective, my bride of twenty-five years of marriage and over twenty-eight years of friendship suffered a sudden and tragic death. At the same time I am confident that because of the grace of God through the shed blood of Jesus Christ in whom she trusted, Tammy did fly away.[1]

As a pastor I know what it's like to tell someone they've lost a loved one. I've been in the hospital room as people have slipped into eternity. I remember sitting by my mom's bedside, watching my dad talk to her although she couldn't respond. A few years later I left my dad in the hospital knowing that the end was near but believing that he would last a few more weeks. No sooner had I returned home than I had to race back to Mississippi and watch as he gasped frantically for his last breath. My wife was with her dad when he died after a long stay in a veteran's hospital. To see him decline in his health and mind was tragic.

Death is a reality all of us must face. When we do, we are given a choice as to how we react. Death is a brutal reality. It is a reminder to us of what sin has cost us. It reminds us of the finality of life. Have you ever noticed how much we talk about "death" while not actually talking about it? We have conversations that include *words* about death—"I've been dying to talk to you," "You're killing me," or "It's to die for." Yet when it comes to the reality of death, we are strangely silent. People refuse to draw up a last will and testament for fear they are sealing their doom.

> **DEATH IS A REALITY ALL OF US MUST FACE. WHEN WE DO, WE ARE GIVEN A CHOICE AS TO HOW WE REACT.**

George Bernard Shaw said, "One out of one dies."[2] At the beginning of our lives, we pass through the darkness of our mother's womb into the light of a delivery room. At the end of life, the darkness of death comes to us before we can see His eternal light.

Anyone who has ever stood by a casket knows the pains of death. We have all watched death take away a precious life. Death is no respecter of age; it claims the young as well as the old. We often say they died too young. But the good news is that death doesn't have the last word.

THE LIFE GIVER

Death knocked on the door of Mary, Martha, and Lazarus one day. It would seem to us that if anyone should have been immune to the sting of death, it would have been the friends of

Jesus. Suddenly, seemingly before his time, Lazarus died. Jesus could have rushed to his side and healed him, but He didn't. And His delay meant the death of a friend.

John 11 is a familiar text. There are truths hidden within to help us when God seems slow or late. Up until this time, Jesus had talked about life. He had revealed Himself as the water of life, the giver of eternal life, the bread of life, the light of life, and the source of abundant life. But in John 11, He revealed Himself as life itself—the essence of life. There is nothing that proves the sufficiency of Christ more than times of death.

Lazarus was sick. In today's prosperity gospel where healing is both expected and demanded of God, Lazarus and his family would have been accused of not having enough faith. Someone might have walked in and said, "He must be sick because of unconfessed sin." Maybe God didn't love Lazarus, or maybe He was incapable of delivering Lazarus from this sickness.

When He was informed of his friend's illness, Jesus didn't respond the way we would expect Him to respond. He waited. He delayed. All the while, desperation grew within the four walls of the house where his friend lay dying.

> When Jesus arrived, He found that Lazarus had already been in the tomb four days. Bethany was near Jerusalem (about two miles away). Many of the Jews had come to Martha and Mary to comfort them about their brother. As soon as Martha heard that Jesus was coming, she went to meet Him. But Mary remained seated in the

house. Then Martha said to Jesus, "Lord, if You had been here, my brother wouldn't have died. Yet even now I know that whatever You ask from God, God will give You."

"Your brother will rise again," Jesus told her. Martha said, "I know that he will rise again in the resurrection at the last day."

Jesus said to her, "I am the resurrection and the life. The one who believes in Me, even if he dies, will live. Everyone who lives and believes in Me will never die—ever. Do you believe this?"

"Yes, Lord," she told him. "I believe You are the Messiah, the Son of God, who was to come into the world."

Having said this, she went back and called her sister Mary, saying in private, "The Teacher is here and is calling for you." As soon as she heard this, she got up quickly and went to Him. Jesus had not yet come into the village but was still in the place where Martha had met Him. The Jews who were with her in the house consoling her saw that Mary got up quickly and went out. So they followed her, supposing that she was going to the tomb to cry there.

When Mary came to where Jesus was and saw Him, she fell at His feet and told Him, "Lord, if You had been here, my brother would not have died!" When Jesus saw her crying, and the Jews who had come with her crying, He was angry in His spirit and deeply moved. "Where have you put him?" He asked.

"Lord," they told Him, "come and see."

Jesus wept. So the Jews said, "See how He loved him!" But some of them said, "Couldn't He who opened the blind man's eyes also have kept this man from dying?"

Then Jesus, angry in Himself again, came to the tomb. It was a cave, and a stone was lying against it. "Remove the stone," Jesus said. Martha, the dead man's sister, told Him, "Lord, he already stinks. It's been four days." Jesus said to her, "Didn't I tell you that if you believed you would see the glory of God?"

So they removed the stone. Then Jesus raised His eyes and said, "Father, I thank You that You heard Me. I know that You always hear Me, but because of the crowd standing here I said this, so they may believe You sent me." After He said this, He shouted with a loud voice, "Lazarus, come out!" The dead man came out bound hand and foot with linen strips and with his face wrapped in cloth. Jesus said to them, "Loose him and let him go."

Therefore many of the Jews who came to Mary and saw what He did believed in Him. But

some of them went to the Pharisees and told
them what Jesus had done. (John 11:17–46)

Often when we go through difficult times, our view of God
can change. We can point fingers, ask a ton of "Why?" questions, and even be tempted to blame God. After all, "If He had
been there, this wouldn't have happened." We all can cave into
the limited perspectives of Mary and Martha. They loved Jesus,
but at that moment their faith was weak and their doubts were
strong.

MORE QUESTIONS THAN ANSWERS

Have you ever been disappointed with God? Have you
ever been desperate for Him to break through in your life in a
miraculous way, only to feel that He sits silently and watches
you suffer? Be honest, all of us have had moments when in our
disappointment or desperation we've wondered if God really
cares.

The Scripture is crystal clear: "Jesus loved Martha, her sister, and Lazarus" (John 11:5). These three had a strong bond
in the Lord. Their home was a place of refuge for Jesus. He
was comfortable there. I think it goes without saying that no
one other than the disciples and His mother meant more to
Jesus. They loved Him. They were loyal followers of the Lord.
Scripture indicates this was a home He visited often. What we
tend to forget is that Jesus was not close by when He got word
that Lazarus was sick. Although the messengers would not have
known this, Lazarus was possibly already dead. When Jesus

finally arrived after a two-day delay, Lazarus would have been dead four days.

Martha met Him first. Mary was too overcome with grief to leave the house. Jesus comforted Martha with the revelation that He is the resurrection and the life. Jesus was telling her, "Death is not final; there is life after death." Martha responded to the revelation by stating truths she believed in her mind. She believed the dead would one day be raised, but Jesus challenged her to believe it in her heart.

Martha said, "I know he will rise one day, but right now he's dead." Jesus responded by saying, in essence, "Not for long!" Assured that the Lord was in control, Martha went to Mary and told her to go see Jesus. Notice that both sisters started their conversations by saying, "If you had been here, things

WHEN YOU CAN'T SEE THE ROAD AHEAD, DO YOU TRUST HIM? WHEN IT DOESN'T ALL MAKE SENSE, DO YOU QUESTION HIM?

would have been different. We wouldn't be going through this. You could have spared us this distress." Obviously these sisters would have talked among themselves, trying to figure out why the Master did not hasten to come to them in their hour of desperation. But Jesus had a greater purpose in mind. God was going to be glorified in this death. The problem wasn't the stench of death but the sting of death. Jesus was stretching them to believe in the greater purposes of God in desperate times.

When you can't see the road ahead, do you trust Him? When it doesn't all make sense, do you question Him? In those moments of desperation, despair, and doubt, God is moving us toward a confession of faith in His sovereign control. Will you trust Him?

Put yourself in Mary's situation. She was a follower of Christ, but she was still human. She was grieving, and Jesus had not come. I'm sure she prayed fervently and desperately for the healing of Lazarus. I'm sure others prayed for his health to be restored. Still the Master had not come. His delay confused her and may have even angered her. It certainly grieved her.

As soon as she heard He was calling for her, she ran to Him. The way, the truth, and the life had come. The One who would reveal Himself as the resurrection and the life had come. The One who will wipe away all tears had come. He had called her. Her name was on His lips.

It seems from the text that Jesus spoke to both of the women outside the town of Bethany. He was able to talk to them alone. His ministry to them was individual and personal. He always meets us in the quiet. He finds us when we are alone, or feeling alone, and there He comforts us. In our distress He brings peace; in our fear He calls us to deepen our faith.

"Lord, if You had been here, my brother wouldn't have died." These are the only words we have from the lips of Mary. In her estimation, it was too late. All hope was gone. Lazarus was dead and decaying. He had been placed in a sealed grave.

A GOD WHO CRIES

John reveals to us Jesus' response when He sees our desperate hearts. "When Jesus saw her crying, and the Jews who had come with her crying, He was angry in His spirit and deeply moved" (John 11:33). Does Jesus care? Can He identify with our sorrow, grief, anguish, and despair?

In his very helpful commentary on this passage, William Barclay writes:

> John had written his whole gospel on the theme that in Jesus we see the mind of God. To the Greek the primary characteristic of God was what he called *apatheia*, which means total inability to feel any emotion whatsoever. How did the Greeks come to attribute such a characteristic to God? They argued like this. If we can feel sorrow or joy, gladness or grief, it means that someone can have an effect upon us. Now, if a person has an effect upon us, it means that for the moment that person has power over us. No one can have any power over God; and this must mean that God is essentially incapable of feeling any emotion whatsoever. The Greeks believed in an isolated, passion-less, and compassionless God. What a different picture Jesus gave. He showed us a God whose heart is wrung with anguish for the anguish of his people. The greatest thing Jesus did was to bring us the news of a God who cares.[3]

Every time you see Mary in the New Testament, she's at the feet of Jesus. Is this where you run when you are desperate?

Do you run *from* God, or *to* God? Do you fall down before Him, or brazenly question His love for you? Mary's response in her desperate hour should be ours as well. I love the way Warren Wiersbe summarizes these verses in his commentary:

> Mary did not say much because she was overcome with sorrow and began to weep. Her friends joined in the weeping, as Jewish people are accustomed to do. The word used means "a loud weeping, a lamentation." Our Lord's response was to groan within and "be moved with indignation." At what was He indignant? At the ravages of sin in the world that He had created. Death is an enemy, and Satan uses the fear of death as a terrible weapon. . . . "Jesus wept" is the shortest and yet the deepest verse in Scripture. His was a silent weeping (the Greek word is used nowhere else in the New Testament) and not the loud lamentation of the mourners. But why did He weep at all? After all, He knew that He would raise Lazarus from the dead (John 11:11). Our Lord's weeping reveals the humanity of the Savior. He has entered into all of our experiences and knows how we feel. In fact, being the perfect God-Man, Jesus experienced these things in a deeper way than we do. His tears also assure us of His sympathy; He is indeed "a Man of sorrows and

acquainted with grief" (Isa. 53:3 NKJV). Today He is our merciful and faithful High Priest, and we may come to the throne of grace and find all the gracious help that we need (see Heb. 4:14–16).[4]

"Jesus wept." I've heard people make fun of that verse. The only thing you ever hear about that verse is that it's the shortest one in the Bible. It may be, but those two words reveal the great depth of the love of God. The great expositor C. H. Spurgeon wrote, "There is infinitely more in these two words than any sermonizer or student of the Word will ever be able to bring out of them, even though he should apply the microscope of the utmost attentive consideration."[5]

God knows when I hurt. He knows the pain I feel.

There are three times when the Scriptures mention that Jesus wept. There were tears of sorrow at the grave of Lazarus; there were tears of sorrow over Jerusalem; there were tears of suffering and agony in Gethsemane. Bethany reminds us that He understands the moments of despair. Jerusalem reminds us that He understands the moments of disappointment. Gethsemane reminds us that He understands the moments of desperation. He is a man of sorrows, acquainted with grief.

NEVER LATE, NEVER LEFT ALONE

We are not alone in desperate times. He met Martha and Mary in their moment of desperation. He was late by their calculations, but He was right on time for a miracle. He spoke the truth to Martha, and it comforted her. He shed tears with Mary, and they comforted her. In both truth and tears, we find the presence of God sufficient. Marcus L. Loane wrote, "Mankind knows no sorrow at all that lies outside the compass of the experience of our Immanuel."[6]

The writer of Hebrews also wrote words of comfort regarding Christ's humanity:

> Now since the children have flesh and blood in common, He also shared in these, so that through His death He might destroy the one holding the power of death—that is, the Devil—and free those who were held in slavery all their lives by the fear of death. For it is clear that He does not reach out to help angels, but to help Abraham's offspring. Therefore He had to be like His brothers in every way, so that He could become a merciful and faithful high priest in service to God, to make propitiation for the sins of the people. For since He Himself was tested and has suffered, He is able to help those who are tested. (2:14–18)

WILL YOU SEE GOD IN THE MIDST OF YOUR CRISIS AND THEN USE THAT CRISIS AS A MINISTRY TO OTHERS?

No matter where you are or what you are going through, God may seem slow, but He is never late. He will be with you every hour of every day. Whatever you are going through, there's a purpose in it. There's a reason for it. It's not a matter of whether or not God is with you; He is there. The issue is this: Will you see God in the midst of your crisis and then use that crisis as a ministry to others?

Paul was well acquainted with affliction, despair, and desperation. But he was even better acquainted with the comfort of God.

> Blessed be the God and Father of our Lord Jesus Christ, the Father of mercies and the God of all comfort. He comforts us in all our affliction, so that we may be able to comfort those who are in any kind of affliction, through the comfort we ourselves receive from God. For as the sufferings of Christ overflow to us, so our comfort overflows through Christ. If we are afflicted, it is for your comfort and salvation; if we are comforted, it is for your comfort, which is experienced in the endurance of the same sufferings that we suffer. And our hope for you is firm, because we know that as you share in the sufferings, so you will share in the comfort.
>
> For we don't want you to be unaware, brothers, of our affliction that took place in the province of Asia; we were completely overwhelmed—beyond our strength—so that we even despaired of life. However, we personally

had a death sentence within ourselves so that we would not trust in ourselves, but in God who raises the dead. He has delivered us from such a terrible death, and He will deliver us; we have placed our hope in Him that He will deliver us again. And you can join in helping with prayer for us, so that thanks may be given by many on our behalf for the gift that came to us through the prayers of many. (2 Cor. 1:3–11)

God will meet you at your point of need so that down the road you can meet someone else in their time of need. We are to pass on what we've learned. We are to be ministers of the mercy of God who, in our moments of great crisis, became our all-sufficient Savior.

In the children's classic *The Velveteen Rabbit*, we learn the story of a stuffed child's toy. Christmas came, and the velveteen rabbit felt lonely and forgotten amid the shiny new mechanical toys. One day he struck up a conversation with the wisest and oldest toy in the house, the skin horse. The velveteen rabbit noticed that the skin horse was worn and aged from much use over time.

"What is real?" the velveteen rabbit asked the skin horse. The skin horse replied, "Real isn't how you are made, it's a thing that happens to you. When a child loves you for a long, long time, not just to play with, but really loves you, then you become Real."

"Does it hurt?" asked the rabbit.

"Sometimes," said the skin horse, "but when you are real, you don't mind being hurt. It doesn't happen all at once, it takes a long time. That's why it doesn't happen often to people who break easily or have sharp edges, or who have to be carefully kept. Generally, by the time you are Real, most of your hair has been loved off, and your eyes drop out and you get loose in the joints and very shabby. But these things don't matter at all, because once you are Real, you can't be ugly, except to people who don't understand."[7]

Much like the classic children's story, those whom the Lord loves are sometimes wounded by Him. Whether as a means of discipline, refining, or glorifying the Father, the wounds make us look more like Christ. Though He wounds, He will heal. "For He has torn us, and He will heal us; He has wounded us, and He will bind up our wounds" (Hosea 6:1). He doesn't merely heal, but He heals us by His own wounds. "But He was pierced because of our transgressions, crushed because of our iniquities; punishment for our peace was on Him, and we are healed by His wounds" (Isa. 53:5).

GOD WILL MEET YOU AT YOUR POINT OF NEED SO THAT DOWN THE ROAD YOU CAN MEET SOMEONE ELSE IN THEIR TIME OF NEED.

So regardless of the situation, no matter how desperate it may seem, remember that the nail-scarred hands bring healing and hope to your scars.

CHAPTER 12

BROKEN AND SPILLED OUT

John 12

The grand design of God in all the afflictions
that befall his people is to bring them nearer
and closer to himself.
—Thomas Brooks

Lord, I call to You; my rock, do not be deaf
to me. If You remain silent to me, I will be
like those going down to the Pit. Listen to the
sound of my pleading when I cry to You for
help, when I lift up my hands toward Your holy
sanctuary.
—Psalm 28:1–2

HAVE YOU EVER BROKEN anything valuable? As a kid, did you pick up a piece of Grandma's fine china and drop it? I did, and she was not happy. I remember another time when we mailed a wedding gift of expensive Waterford crystal to a couple. It arrived broken and worthless.

I have a small oil lamp I bought in Jerusalem a few years ago. There is not a crack in it. I could have gotten one with a small corner broken off for pennies on the dollar, but I wanted the unbroken one. It was more valuable and more impressive. With that small lamp, a room in a first-century home could be lit. Although made of clay, it is very valuable.

In our minds, broken things lose their value, unless you are operating from heaven's perspective. It seems God values broken things. It was true in the story of the potter and the clay. God doesn't toss aside broken things, He remakes them and uses them for His glory. As believers we need to be reminded of this truth. Often God allows defeat, setback, adversity, or tragedy to bring us to the end of self. In the process He makes us more and more like Christ, and self is sifted out.

Brokenness is the forgotten blessing for the believer. When we are broken, we give to God that which the world views as worthless, and He makes it priceless. God takes broken people and uses them as trophies of grace. He takes a prostitute, brings her to desperation, and in turn she finds a way to minister to others who have made immoral choices. He takes a drunkard and turns his life around so others can see the transforming power of the gospel.

None of us would ever choose to be broken. We want a

smooth road with no bumps or potholes. Like it or not, it's the pruning, the breaking, the cutting back, and the humbling that mark us and give our testimonies credibility. Anyone can praise God in the good times, but praising Him in the storm is another thing altogether.

The thought of brokenness frightens us, in fact, but God uses it for great gain. Stuart Briscoe notes, "There is a sovereign Lord from whom we come, through whom we live, by whom we survive and to whom we are accountable. And he is himself the source of all that is of value. It is in relationship to this sovereign Lord that we find our system of values. It is through the spiritual life this Son gives and through the ministry of the Holy Spirit that we can gain insight into these values, as well as obtain the power to put them into practice."[1]

God sometimes takes "good" people and rocks their world. He calls for a season of breaking and desperation. It is not God's design to destroy but to produce lives of worship and witness in those who yield to Him.

ALL-WEATHER TRIALS

I've watched this happen with two dear friends. I first met Harris when he was pastor of a church in a nearby community. His wife, Phyllis, and I served for several years together on the Southern Baptist Convention's Foreign Mission Board (now known as the International Mission Board). Harris recently accepted a position with the Georgia Baptist Convention that enables him to travel all over southwest Georgia ministering to and encouraging pastors.

If you have seen Sherwood Pictures' film *Fireproof*, then you'll recognize my friends. They play Caleb Holt's parents in the movie. Harris and Phyllis exceptionally portray the roles of loving parents who want their son to know the love of Christ they have experienced for themselves.

Here's a couple who "had it all." Harris was pastor of the First Baptist Church in a county-seat town. He was loved and respected. But in one moment his and Phyliss's world was turned upside down . . . twice. As you read their story, you'll sense how two desperate situations brought them closer to Jesus than they had ever been. Read carefully what God taught them through their times of brokenness.

In February 2000 the worst tornado in fifty-three years struck Mitchell and Grady counties in Georgia. Harris and Phyllis and their sixteen-year-old daughter were asleep in bed. Phyllis was awakened by the increasingly strong winds and hail battering their house. The family had only a few short moments to huddle under a mattress in the hallway. When the storm had passed, only the roof over their heads was left on their demolished home.

Immediately the family recognized God's provision and protection. Due to the high speed of the winds, they believe God sent angels to hold the mattress down over their heads. When they emerged from the rubble, their daughter walked over broken glass and debris without shoes and wasn't injured. Miraculously a tree fell on their house in the shape of a cross, and it pointed the way out of the mess.

Their first thought after the tornado was, *We're alive!*

Though they felt helpless, they said the presence of God during those moments was palpably real. Being a pastor, Harris soon began to wonder how to minister to others in desperate circumstances when he himself was so desperate. He struggled with guilt as other church members faced the same plight, but he knew he had a responsibility to his own family first. Harris said his quiet times became long periods of silence and solitude comprised of groanings too deep for words.

Many have asked them, "Where was God during that tornado?" Their response: "Right in the middle of the storm with us." This family recognizes that God sends rain on both the just and the unjust. Phyllis said, "If you ride out the storm with God, you're never the same again." Their desperate situation drove them to a greater hunger for the Lord, and they got to know Him in a more intimate way than ever before.

But that was only the beginning.

A year after the tornado, Phyllis was diagnosed with breast cancer. Once again the family found themselves desperate and overwhelmed. Phyllis said that in addition to physical healing, she needed God to heal her heart. She ached with the pain and fear of an uncertain future. God used the words of Psalm 28 to bring that spiritual and emotional healing: "LORD, I call to You; my rock, do not be deaf to me. If You remain silent to me, I will be like those going down to the Pit. Listen to the sound of my pleading when I cry to You for help, when I lift up my hands toward Your holy sanctuary. . . . May the LORD be praised, for He has heard the sound of my pleading. The LORD is my strength and my shield; my heart trusts in Him, and I am helped. Therefore my heart rejoices, and I praise Him with my song" (vv. 1–2, 6–7).

Harris faced Phyllis's cancer differently. He said he would hold Phyllis at night while she cried, feeling so helpless. He prayed what felt like inadequate prayers and was forced to wait on the Lord. And the Lord showed up. He touched Phyllis one day and calmed her anxious heart. But Phyllis knew He had also brought physical healing to her body. She said to the Lord, "What do I do now?" And she sensed Him say, "Get up and act like it."

Phyllis said, "When Jesus speaks, things change. He is enough." She did receive a clean report from doctors, and she testified of the goodness and grace of the Lord. She realized that the world doesn't really care how you act during the good times, but they do watch when things are tough.

This family realizes that God never wastes an experience, a pit, or a pain. Though they faced many desperate circumstances, they are grateful for all the Lord has brought them through. Harris noted, "So often our desperation is 'until' something happens. We won't get desperate for God until we're forced to. But there needs to come a time when we maintain a constant posture of desperation." Unfortunately many people don't learn during trials, as this couple did, because they allow the enemy to turn those trials into temptations to curse God or wallow in despair.

George Mueller, the great man of faith, once said, "There was a day when I died to George Mueller; his opinions and preferences, taste and will; died to the world, its approval or censure; died to the approval or blame even of my brethren or friends, and since then I have striven only to show myself approved unto God."[2]

THE BREAKING POINT

In John 12 we find an incredible story of a nobody we'll never forget. She didn't set out to be a star; she simply wanted to love and obey the Lord. She didn't try to draw attention to herself and was praised by some while criticized by others. The bottom line is that she was honored by Christ. Broken people will always find favor with God.

> Six days before the Passover, Jesus came to Bethany where Lazarus was, the one Jesus had raised from the dead. So they gave a dinner for Him there; Martha was serving them, and Lazarus was one of those reclining at the table with Him. Then Mary took a pound of fragrant oil—pure and expensive nard—anointed Jesus' feet, and wiped His feet with her hair. So the house was filled with the fragrance of the oil.
>
> Then one of His disciples, Judas Iscariot (who was about to betray Him), said, "Why wasn't this fragrant oil sold for 300 denarii and given to the poor?" He didn't say this because he cared about the poor but because he was a thief. He was in charge of the money bag and would steal part of what was put in it.

Jesus answered, "Leave her alone; she has kept it for the day of My burial. For you always have the poor with you, but you do not always have Me." (vv. 1–8)

God values things we scoff at. Mary poured out the ointment on her Lord. This was the first century when women were supposed to be seen and not heard. She slipped in quietly and anointed her Master with costly perfume. Most in the room rebuked her, but Jesus praised her. Judas, the ultimate prosperity preacher, basically said, "What a waste. We could have used that money for the ministry. Why would anyone do something so stupid?" Of course, Judas would have been against any sign of sacrifice because he was a thief. He wasn't interested in Jesus and certainly didn't comprehend sacrifice on this level.

> **ONE REASON MANY PEOPLE ARE UNWILLING TO BE BROKEN IS BECAUSE THEY KNOW THE PRICE OF EVERYTHING AND THE VALUE OF NOTHING.**

As a pastor I often find people who cannot comprehend sacrificial giving to church projects or missions. They can't imagine or envision anyone giving up something significant, personal, or valuable for the cause of Christ. Why? Like Judas, they have a selfish, thieving heart. They are only interested in Christ for what they can get from Him. They have no heart for God's glory and no vision for a dying world. But they scoff at those who sacrifice while still wanting to enjoy all the blessings and privileges that are afforded them because of others' sacrificial spirit.

Mary's first move was an act of loving sacrifice. Can't you picture the scene in your mind? Mary comes into the room with the jar of expensive perfume as Jesus is reclining on the couch. She breaks the jar and pours its contents on His head and feet, wiping them with her own crown of glory, her hair. It is a beautiful act, one that captures the attention of all who are present.

Not only was Judas outraged, but Mark's account also tells us that others at the house responded the same way. One reason many people are unwilling to be broken is because they know the price of everything and the value of nothing. God has a different set of scales, and He weighs by different measures. Nothing offends religious people more than someone showing them up, especially when that person is sincere.

What Mary did was not wasteful; it was an act of worship—unlike some of the expressions and activities we call "worship" today. That's because there can be no real worship without surrender, brokenness, and yielding. To stand before an audience of One, you have to come knowing you are nothing and that He alone is worthy of praise.

God always seems to make note of extravagant worship. The word "extravagant" means to exceed what is reasonable or appropriate, to be lavish and unrestrained. It paints a picture of exceeding the limits. Extravagant worship is elaborate and expressive. It goes far beyond what most believers in America can fathom. God forbid that we still hold Sunday night services and prayer meetings! Who has that much time to give to God?

Several years ago I took my family to New York City for Christmas. We splurged and stayed at the Plaza Hotel (in the cheapest room we could find). We ate at our favorite restaurants and saw several shows. On Christmas Eve we made our way to the Brooklyn Tabernacle for their worship service and stayed for their Christmas cantata. Pastor Jim Cymbala preached a powerful sermon that day and, as I recall, about 125 people came down the aisle to receive Christ.

When we left, we walked into freezing weather and a bitterly strong wind. We turned the corner and saw a line of hundreds of people waiting to get in the church for the next performance. They were standing with Christmas packages in hand, singing carols. Those at the front of the line had been outside in the cold for nearly two hours. One lady asked me, "How many were saved? Did anybody come to Jesus today?" They were freezing on Christmas Eve, but they were singing carols, praising God, and wanting to know if people's lives had been changed.

I was stunned. I've been in church all my life. I've preached in churches all across this nation. In most places people are more prone to gripe than to glory in what God is doing. They whine instead of worship. I asked myself why there was such a difference. Then it hit me—they've never gotten over their salvation.

The Brooklyn Tabernacle is full of people saved out of drugs, prostitution, gangs, and homosexuality. They got saved, and they've never gotten over it. God has blessed that church with an incredible facility because the members are willing to sacrifice. They were broken by sin and headed to hell, but now they are blessed by God and willing to be a blessing to others.

What God has done through the ministry of the Brooklyn Tabernacle is nothing short of miraculous. The church is not made up of Wall Street executives and power brokers. Its members have been delivered from the wisdom of this world and have given their lives to the foolishness of the gospel.

Please don't miss what Jesus said in regard to Mary's sacrifice and the reaction of others to it. He told those who judged her to back off. Jesus always has

BROKEN PEOPLE LOOK FOR WAYS TO BE A BLESSING. THEY ARE NOT STORAGE FACILITIES; THEY ARE DELIVERY SYSTEMS.

an issue with religious people. They never want to sacrifice or invest for the sake of the kingdom. They just want to tell others how they should use their money and talents. They take but never give. Mary's gift was extravagant. It was costly, pure nard, worth about a year's salary for a common worker. And remember, God didn't ask her to do it; she willingly lavished what she had on Christ.

This was a once-in-a-lifetime opportunity. Jesus had set His face to Jerusalem and would soon be crucified. Mary seized the moment. Broken people look for ways to be a blessing. They are not storage facilities; they are delivery systems. Broken people are like an artesian well. They just keep finding ways to pour out their lives on others.

In his commentary on Mark, Ray Stedman writes, "I am sure our Lord calls attention to this aspect of her gift of love because it is such a practical lesson for all of us: use what you have and do what you can. You cannot feed the starving world, but you can feed one person. You cannot evangelize the whole world, but you can share the gospel story with the people around you. You can't comfort all the lonely people on earth, but you can comfort one or two. So do as Mary did: use what you have and do what you can."[3]

While the disciples and the guests in the house were trying to figure out what Mary was thinking, Jesus knew her heart. She was preparing His body for burial. Broken people are sensitive to the moment. They are tenderhearted. They see and hear with spiritual eyes and ears. Of all those who reclined at the table, only Mary was sensitive enough to do something sacrificial for the Savior.

Notice what Jesus said to the crowd in Mark's gospel: "She has done what she could; she has anointed My body in advance for burial. I assure you: Wherever the gospel is proclaimed in the whole world, what this woman has done will also be told in memory of her" (14:8–9). I'm sure this is not what Mary had in mind. She wasn't looking for recognition or reward. She was just offering the sacrifices of worship to her Lord. We can never fully measure or comprehend how God might use our broken lives for His glory and for the gospel.

FREE TO GIVE, FREE TO LIVE

We may not think much of giving a cup of cold water or of visiting someone in prison, but Jesus does. He notices the small things that pass the attention of the casual onlooker. He watches the treasury and sees the widow's mite. He sees the prayer made in secret. We may not know until eternity how our afflictions, brokenness, and sacrifices were used to further the gospel.

Who would have ever thought a little jar of pure nard would draw so much attention? While the perfume would have filled the room with a strong fragrance at the time, no one would have expected its aroma to still rise from the pages of Scripture two thousand years later. While much of what happened in those thirty-three years of earthly ministry is forgotten in the dust of history, the aroma of a small jar from a simple woman remains.

Why did she do it? She acted out of the overflow of her gratitude and love for Christ. It was the best way she could express her worship, devotion, and love in that hour. She didn't ask to give a speech. She didn't write a book. She poured out her perfume, the very best she had. In those days kings were often anointed at a banquet in their honor. The bottle was broken to reveal the depths of her devotion to Christ.

In a similar account in Luke 7, Jesus gives further insight into the motivation behind such an extravagant act of worship. "Therefore I tell you, her many sins have been forgiven; that's why she loved much. But the one who is forgiven little, loves little" (v. 47). Most commentators believe the account recorded here is different from the one recorded in John 12. We can say with a great deal of certainty, however, that Mary had been forgiven by Jesus. When we have been delivered from the power and penalty of sin in a time of desperation, our worship before the Lord will be outrageous and extravagant.

This anointing in John 12 was an act of absolute surrender. The alabaster jar was made of translucent stone. Once the lid was broken, everything had to be used. Nothing could be held back. This type of sacrificial worship demands devotion, not calculation. It reveals itself in a selfless, spontaneous, and eternal act.

Who knows how far that aroma has spread? It has permeated cultures, tribes, nations, and tongues all across the world. It has been printed in hundreds of languages and told by tens of thousands of believers. It has been taught by countless pastors and Sunday school teachers. The fragrance still fills the room.

The need of the hour is for available, surrendered worshippers of Christ. We need people willing to give of themselves, willing to be broken and spilled out and poured at His feet. We have training, programs, and events, but where's the aroma of a broken life? We have bells and whistles, but where is the fragrance of sacrifice? Where is the truth that drifts through the air and causes people to want to breathe it in? The condition for blessing is found in brokenness and surrender.

For Harris and Phyllis, it all came down to Jesus. Nothing else mattered. Their lives are a fragrance of Christ wherever they go. Harris is still ministering to pastors throughout our region. I look at them when I'm preaching and think of the sweet aroma of Christ that surrounds their lives. As long as the Lord tarries, the work they have done as pastor, pastor's wife, denominational servants, friends of sinners, and actors in a movie will bear fruit that remains.

That's the power of desperation.

ACKNOWLEDGMENTS

I must express my appreciation to Thomas Walters and the entire team at B&H Publishing Group for believing in me and in this project. Without their support, prayers, and input, this would not be the book it is today. Many people whose names you will never know have played a vital part in polishing and publishing this book.

Once again I must thank my assistant, Debbie Toole, who manages my life and my calendar. She keeps me on track and makes sure I'm where I'm supposed to be when I'm supposed to be there. My research assistant, Stephanie Bennett, has again helped me in pulling material together, doing interviews, and editing the manuscript. She has been very patient with me and has worked to help us make every deadline.

Without an incredible and understanding wife, this project would not be possible. Terri has given me the time (often late at night) to think and write. She has provided input and has prayed for me as I've tried to meet deadlines. She is God's gift to me, and she's my best friend. I'm grateful for both our daughters, Erin and Hayley, who as adults serve God in their areas of giftedness. To be called their dad is one of the greatest honors I have ever known.

Many have encouraged me in this project and in writing in general. In the last few years, Sherwood Baptist Church, where I am privileged to pastor, has seen a multitude of blessings from on high. God has met us in our desperation to be a different church with a ministry that is not status quo. We've tasted revival. We've seen the wind of the Spirit blow and the mercy drops of awakening in our midst.

Through Sherwood Pictures™ we've been able to touch the world from Albany, Georgia. Today the ministry of Sherwood is impacting the world as our movies have been translated into thirteen languages and are on every continent on the planet. I am blessed to be a small part of what God is doing through our films. Through our ReFRESH Conferences™ we have been able to touch hundreds of pastors and layleaders in their times of desperation. These ministries would not be possible without a supportive church and an incredible staff.

Tom and Jeannie Elliff have become dear friends to me over the past few years. Tom has given me wise counsel and encouraged me to want to be more like Jesus. Every time I hear him preach, I'm convicted of how much more of Jesus I need. I am grateful for Tom's willingness to write the foreword.

When Jimmy Draper was president of LifeWay Christian

Resources, he encouraged me to start writing. At that time I was just writing articles for our church newsletter. His notes of encouragement have been a blessing to me. I owe much of who I am to the man we Southern Baptists affectionately call "Brother Jimmy."

There are others who have believed in me through the years. Space does not allow me to mention all of them. It is because of these people, however—both laity and ministers—that I am who I am today. Some you would know, and others you will not know until glory. Yet all of them have been used by God to prune me, teach me, pray for me, and encourage me. I am forever indebted to the "others" who have ministered to me.

Most of all I am grateful to the Lord Jesus who has shown incredible patience with me and has loved me unconditionally. There are others more qualified to write on this subject. I just want to be available to be used by Him. If what I have shared in this book blesses you, give the praise where it belongs, to my Lord and Savior Jesus Christ.

— **Michael Catt**

NOTES

CHAPTER 1

1. Theodore Epp, *The God of Abraham, Isaac and Jacob* (Lincoln, NE: Back to the Bible, 1970), 210–11.

2. A. W. Tozer, *The Knowledge of the Holy* (San Francisco: Harper & Row, 1961), 6–7.

3. Lloyd John Ogilvie, *Lord of the Impossible* (Nashville: Abingdon, 1984), 29.

4. Gene Getz, *Jacob: Following God without Looking Back* (Nashville: Broadman & Holman, 1996), 143–44.

CHAPTER 2

1. Robert Bailey, *The Wilderness Experience* (Nashville: Broadman, 1989), 12.

2. Josiah H. Gilbert, *Three Thousand Selected Quotes from Brilliant Writers* (Hartford, CT: S. S. Scranton, 1914), 329.

3. John Blanchard, *The Complete Gathered Gold* (Webster, NY: Evangelical Press, 2006), 319.
4. Warren Wiersbe, *The Bible Exposition Commentary: Old Testament, 2001–2004* (accessed via *PC Study Bible*).
5. Stuart Briscoe, "Perils of the Good Life" (Telling the Truth Ministries, CD).
6. Ruth Bell Graham, *Prodigals and Those Who Love Them* (Grand Rapids: Baker, 1991).
7. Thomas Merton, *Thoughts in Solitude* (New York: Dell, 1961), 25–26.

CHAPTER 3

1. Jill Briscoe, *A Little Pot of Oil: A Life Overflowing* (Colorado Springs: Multnomah, 2003), 9.
2. A. W. Pink, *Gleanings from Elisha* (Chicago: Moody, 1972), 62.
3. A. W. Tozer, *How to Be Filled with the Holy Spirit* (Harrisburg, PA: Christian Publications), 19.
4. George Duncan, *It Could Be Your Problem* (London: Pickering & Inglis, 1977), 39.
5. A. W. Pink, *Gleanings from Elisha*, 63.
6. Jill Briscoe, *A Little Pot of Oil*, 36.

CHAPTER 4

1. T. S. Rendall, *Elisha: Prophet of the Abundant Life* (Three Hills, AB, Canada: Prairie Bible Institute, 1969), 169.
2. David Roper, *Seasoned with Salt: Lessons from Elisha* (Grand Rapids: Discovery House, 2004), 86.

3. Ron Dunn, "Trust and Obey" (Irving, TX: Lifestyle Ministries, 2003), used by permission.

4. C. H. Spurgeon, "Mr. Evil-Questioning Tried and Executed," www.spurgeon.org/sermons/0297.htm (accessed July 18, 2008).

5. Warren Wiersbe, *The Bible Exposition Commentary: Old Testament, 2001–2004* (accessed via *PC Study Bible*).

6. David Jeremiah, *Slaying the Giants in Your Life* (Nashville: Word, 2001), 153–54.

CHAPTER 5

1. Jim Cymbala, *Fresh Wind, Fresh Fire* (Grand Rapids: Zondervan, 1997).

2. Lamoyne Sharpe, *Preaching through the Psalms: Volume 2* (Lamoyne Sharpe, 1982), 78.

3. Jim Cymbala, *Fresh Wind, Fresh Fire*, 63–65.

CHAPTER 6

1. William MacDonald, *Lord, Break Me!* (Kansas City: Walterick Publishers, 1972), 4.

2. John Oxenham, *Bees in Amber* (London: Methuen & Company, 1936).

3. G. Campbell Morgan, *Student Survey of the Bible* (Chattanooga: AMG, 1993), 235–37.

4. Vance Havner, *Seasonings* (Westwood, NJ: Fleming H. Revell Company, 1970), 12.

5. Donald Grey Barnhouse, *Expositions of Bible Doctrines* (Grand Rapids: Eerdmans, 1966).

CHAPTER 7

1. Vance Havner, *Though I Walk Through the Valley* (Westwood, NJ: Revell, 1974), 5.

2. John Blanchard, *The Complete Gathered Gold* (Webster, NY: Evangelical Press, 2006), 647.

3. Karl A. Slaikeu and Steve Lawhead, *Up from the Ashes* (Grand Rapids: Zondervan, 1987), 5.

4. Glen Van Ekeren, *Speaker's Sourcebook 2* (Upper Saddle River, NJ: Prentice Hall, 1994), 157.

5. George Duncan, *Mastery in the Storm* (London: Lutterworth, 1965), 46.

CHAPTER 8

1. John Laidlaw, *The Miracles of Our Lord* (Grand Rapids: Baker, 1956), 229

2. "Starvation," www.healthatoz.com/healthatoz/Atoz/common/standard/transform.jsp?requestURI=/healthatoz/Atoz/ency/starvation.jsp (accessed July 30, 2008).

3. See www.starvation.net (accessed July 30, 2008).

4. Leslie Flynn, *The Miracles of Jesus* (Wheaton, IL: Victor, 1990), 93.

5. Clovis Chappell, *Sermons from the Miracles* (New York: Abingdon Cokesbury, 1937), 155.

6. Judith Viorst, *Alexander and the Terrible, Horrible, No Good, Very Bad Day* (New York: Scholastic, 1992).

7. David Redding, *The Miracles of Christ* (Westwood, NJ: Revell, 1964), 87.

8. Ibid., 88.

CHAPTER 9

1. Kent Hughes, *Mark: Jesus, Servant and Savior* (Wheaton, IL: Crossway, 1989).

2. A. T. Robertson, *Robertson's Word Pictures in the New Testament* (Broadman, 1985), electronic database.

3. A. W. Tozer, *God Tells the Man Who Cares* (Harrisburg, PA: Christian Publications, 2007), 206–7.

4. Ivor Powell, *Mark's Superb Gospel* (Grand Rapids: Kregel, 1985), 240.

5. John Blanchard, *The Complete Gathered Gold* (Webster, NY: Evangelical Press, 2006), 623.

6. Ibid., 643.

7. C. H. Spurgeon, *Spurgeon at His Best* (Grand Rapids: Baker, 1988), 60.

8. A. E. J. Rawlinson, *Westminster Commentaries: St. Mark* (London: Methuen & Company, 1931), 124.

9. A. T. Robertson, *Studies in Mark's Gospel* (Nashville: Broadman, 1958), 49–50.

10. Oswald Chambers, *Oswald Chambers: The Best from All His Books* (Nashville: Thomas Nelson, 1987), 17.

CHAPTER 10

1. "I Hear the Lord Passing By," words and music by Tim Sheppard © 2006 Tim Sheppard Music Co. (ASCAP). All rights reserved. Used by permission.

2. Vance Havner, *Reflections on the Gospel* (Ft. Washington, PA: Christian Literature Crusade, 2006), 158.

CHAPTER 11

1. See http://elitton.blogspot.com/2007_08_01_archive.html.

2. John Blanchard, *The Complete Gathered Gold* (Webster, NY: Evangelical Press, 2006), 135.

3. William Barclay, *The Daily Study Bible: The Gospel of John, Volume 2* (Edinburgh: St. Andrew, 1975).

4. Warren Wiersbe, *The Bible Exposition Commentary: New Testament, 2001–2004* (accessed via *PC Study Bible*).

5. C. H. Spurgeon, *Metropolitan Tabernacle Pulpit, Vol. 35,* "Jesus Wept" (London: Banner of Truth Trust, 1970), 338.

6. Marcus L. Loane, *Mary of Bethany* (London: Marshall, Morgan & Scott, 1949), 68.

7. Margery Williams, *The Velveteen Rabbit* (Garden City, NY: Doubleday & Company, 1958), http://digital.library.upenn.edu/women/williams/rabbit/rabbit.html (accessed July 31, 2008).

CHAPTER 12

1. Stuart Briscoe, *Choices for a Lifetime* (Carol Stream, IL: Tyndale, 1995), 20.

2. John Blanchard, *The Complete Gathered Gold* (Webster, NY: Evangelical Press, 2006), 570–71.

3. Ray Stedman, *The Servant Who Rules* (Grand Rapids: Discovery House, 2002).

WEB SITES

For more information on Michael Catt, Sherwood Baptist
Church, and their various ministry resources, visit any of these
helpful on-line opportunities.

www.SherwoodBaptist.net

Watch services on-line, read Michael's weekly column, or
purchase messages and resources to encourage and challenge
you in your walk with Christ.

www.ReFRESHConference.org

This conference is hosted twice a year for those who thirst
for revival. ReFRESH™ provides a time of Bible teaching,
encouragement from other pastors and layleaders, and renewal
to keep pressing on. Visit to find out how you can attend.

www.2ProphetU.com

Developed by Michael Catt and Warren Wiersbe, *2ProphetU* is a Web-based magazine published twice a month, featuring articles, sermon outlines, illustrations, Web resources, book reviews, and much more. Membership is free.

www.SherwoodPictures.com

Find the latest information about Sherwood Pictures' movie projects, site licenses, and products from your favorite films.

www.VanceHavner.com

This site is devoted to keeping the name and ministry of Vance Havner alive. Includes articles, sermons, devotionals, and other resources from one of the greatest evangelists and preachers of the twentieth century.

www.RonDunn.com

This site honors the life and ministry of Ron Dunn. Includes audio sermons, articles, and sermon outlines, plus many other valuable resources.